Meditations
on the Cross

Meditations on the Cross

DIETRICH BONHOEFFER

Edited by Manfred Weber

Translated by
Douglas W. Stott

Westminster John Knox Press
Louisville, Kentucky

Translated by Douglas W. Stott
from *Das Außerordentliche wird Ereignis: Kreuz und Auferstehung,*
published 1996 by Kaiser/Gütersloher Verlagshaus, Gütersloh, Germany.

© 1996 Kaiser/Gütersloher Verlagshaus, in Gütersloh.
English translation © Westminster John Knox Press 1998

Scripture quotations from the New Revised Standard Version
of the Bible are copyright © 1989 by the Division of Christian Education
of the National Council of the Churches of Christ in the U.S.A.
and are used by permission.

Publisher's Note: The publication of this work was made possible through
the assistance of INTER NATIONES, Bonn. / Die Herausgabe dieses
Werkes wurde aus Mitteln von INTER NATIONES, Bonn, gefördert.

Book design by Jennifer K. Cox
Cover design by Adhawks

First edition
Published by Westminster John Knox Press
Louisville, Kentucky

This volume draws on material from *Dietrich Bonhoeffer Werke*, which is being translated
and published by Fortress Press. This translation has been reviewed by the Editorial Board
of the English edition but may not be identical to that forthcoming text.

This book is printed on acid-free paper that meets the
American National Standards Institute Z39.48 standard. ♾

PRINTED IN THE UNITED STATES OF AMERICA
02 03 04 05 06 07 — 10 9 8 7 6

Library of Congress Cataloging-in-Publication Data

Bonhoeffer, Dietrich, 1906–1945.
[Ausserordentliche wird Ereignis. English]
Meditations on the Cross / Dietrich Bonhoeffer ; edited by Manfred
Weber ; translated by Douglas W. Stott. — 1st ed.
p.   cm.
Includes bibliographical references.
ISBN 0-664-25755-0
1. Jesus Christ—Crucifixion.   2. Jesus Christ—Resurrection.
3. Jesus Christ—Devotional literature.   4. Lent—Miscellanea.
5. Easter—Miscellanea.   I. Weber, Manfred, 1938– .   II. Title.
BT453.B6613   1998
232.96—dc21   98-29636

Contents

Foreword   vii

Abbreviations   ix

Encountering the Extraordinary   1

Back to the Cross   3

The Path of God   6

Passiontide   9

Discipleship and the Cross   11

Good Friday   20

Worldliness   21

God's Love for Human Beings   23

Truthfulness   24

Suffering in Solidarity   25

On Suffering   27

Limits   28

Cain   29

Judas   31

Conversion   38

Treasures of Suffering   39

Disappointments   46

Ecce Homo   47

Christians and Pagans   60

Hope   62

The Beginning   63

Resurrection   64

Easter   68

Resurrection Instead of Immortality   69

Fate   75

Incarnation—Cross—Resurrection   76

Tension   79

The Visible Community of Faith   80

God in the Midst of Life   85

Notes   91

Foreword

Cross and resurrection, suffering and the overcoming of death were central themes in Dietrich Bonhoeffer's exegetical and theological work. Again and again during his lifetime (1906–1945), he focused on these themes, trying to disclose their relevance for human life and actions, and to answer the question regarding just what Christian life really is.

The following selection of texts not only provides access to the events of Passion and Easter, but also strengthens our assurance and hope that, through the cross and resurrection, Christ addresses us at the very center of our lives and in fact does not abandon us in our discipleship.

The textual interludes, which except in two instances are taken from Bonhoeffer's own letters, illuminate possible existential implications of this situation.

All texts are based on the versions established for the new German edition of Dietrich Bonhoeffer's *Werke,* by consulting the original manuscripts and writings, although the present translation is not connected in any way with the *Dietrich Bonhoeffer Works,* the authorized English Edition of the *Werke.* The footnotes correspond to those in the collected *Werke,* though only the most important (with new numbering) have been selected for this edition.

I would like to thank Dr. Ilse Tödt, Dr. Herbert Anzinger, and Professor Eberhard Bethge for help and encouragement.

Manfred Weber

Abbreviations

Gen.	Genesis
Ex.	Exodus
Lev.	Leviticus
Ezek.	Ezekiel
Isa.	Isaiah
Ps.	Psalms
Matt.	Matthew
Rom.	Romans
1–2 Cor.	1 and 2 Corinthians
Gal.	Galatians
Phil.	Philippians
Col.	Colossians
Heb.	Hebrews
Rev.	Revelation

Encountering the Extraordinary

What is the "extraordinary"? It is the love of Jesus Christ himself, love that goes to the cross in suffering obedience. It is the cross. The peculiar feature of Christian life is precisely this cross, a cross enabling Christians to be beyond the world, as it were, thereby granting them victory over the world. Suffering encountered in the love of the one who is crucified—*that* is the "extraordinary" in Christian existence.

The extraordinary is without doubt that visible element over which the Father in heaven is praised. It cannot remain hidden; people must see it. The worshiping community of Jesus' followers, the congregation of a better righteousness, is the visible congregation that has stepped out of the order of this world and has abandoned everything for the sake of gaining the cross of Christ.

What is the peculiar thing you are *doing*? The extraordinary—and this is the most scandalous thing—is something the disciples *do*. It must be done—just like that better righteousness—and must be done visibly. Not, however, with ethical rigor, nor in any eccentricity of a Christian lifestyle, but in whole-hearted Christian obedience to Jesus' will. The activity will prove to be "peculiar" by leading the active person into Christ's own passion. This activity itself is perpetual suffering and enduring. In it, Christ is suffered by his disciple. If this is not the case, it is not the activity Jesus intended.

In this way, the "extraordinary" is the fulfilling of the law, the keeping of the commandments. In Christ the Crucified and in his congregation, the "extraordinary" becomes an event.

From: "The Sermon on the Mount. Matthew 5," in [The Cost of] *Discipleship*
Preliminary version: London 1934/1935
Final version: Finkenwalde (Pomerania), Theological Seminary, 1936/1937

Back to the Cross

Matthew 17:1–9: Six days later, Jesus took with him Peter and James and his brother John and led them up a high mountain, by themselves. And he was transfigured before them, and his face shone like the sun, and his clothes became dazzling white. Suddenly there appeared to them Moses and Elijah, talking with him. Then Peter said to Jesus, "Lord, it is good for us to be here; if you wish, we will make three dwellings here, one for you, one for Moses, and one for Elijah." While he was still speaking, suddenly a bright cloud overshadowed them, and from the cloud a voice said, "This is my beloved son; with him I am well pleased; listen to him!" When the disciples heard this, they fell to the ground and were overcome by fear. But Jesus came and touched them, saying, "Get up and do not be afraid." And when they looked up, they saw no one except Jesus himself alone. As they were coming down the mountain, Jesus ordered them, "Tell no one about the vision until after the Son of Man has been raised from the dead."

1. Before Jesus leads his disciples into suffering, humiliation, disgrace, and disdain, he summons them and shows himself to them as the Lord in God's glory. Before the disciples must descend with Jesus into the abyss of human guilt, malice, and hatred, Jesus leads them onto a high mountain from which they are to receive help.[1] Before Jesus' face is beaten and spat upon, before his cloak is torn and splattered with blood, the disciples are to see him in his divine glory. His face shines like the face of God, and light is the garment he wears.[2] It is a great blessing that the same disciples who are going to experience Jesus' suffering in Gethsemane are now allowed to see him as the transfigured Son

of God, as the eternal God. The disciples thus go to the cross already knowing about the resurrection, and in this they are *exactly* like us. This knowledge should enable us to bear the cross.

2. Moses and Elijah stand next to the transfigured Jesus: Law and prophecy honor him. They speak with him. Luke says they speak with him "about his departure."[3] What are they to do other than repeat their witness to Christ and see that here it has become true and real? They talk about the cross, about God's mysteries. The Old and New Testaments meet in the light of the transfiguration and speak together. The promise has now been fulfilled. Everything has come to an end.

3. Although the disciples are permitted to see this end, it is Jesus who lets them see it. But now they themselves try to seize it, and want to preserve it. They want to stay in the world of the transfiguration, and no longer want to return to the real world of death. They want to remain in the world of Jesus' visible glory and visible power, in the world of the visible fulfillment of the promise. They want to remain where they can see, and no longer want to return to the world where they cannot see what they believe. And so also is our own reaction upon hearing about the resurrection. We no longer want to return. We want Jesus as the visibly resurrected one, as the splendid, transfigured Jesus. We want his visible power and glory, and we no longer want to return to the cross, to believing against all appearances, to suffering in faith . . . it is good here . . . let us make dwellings.[4]

4. The disciples are not allowed to do this. God's glory comes quite near in the radiant cloud of God's presence, and the Father's voice says: *"This is my beloved son; listen to him!"* They are supposed to hear and to obey him. And so that they indeed can do that, they are shown this glory. The message of the resurrection is there that we might obey the Lord Jesus in life. There is no abiding in and enjoying his visible glory here. Whoever recognizes the transfigured Jesus, whoever recognizes Jesus as God, must also immediately recognize him as well as the cruci-

fied human being, and should hear him, obey him. Luther's vision of Christ: "the crucified Lord!"

5. Now the disciples are overcome by fear. Now they comprehend what is going on. They were, after all, still in the world, unable to bear such glory. They sinned against God's glory. Jesus then comes to them, touches them. He is their Lord. He is the living Lord. He stays with them. He leads them back into the world in which both he and they must still live.

6. This is why that image of glory must now recede. "And they saw no one except Jesus himself alone"—just as they had known him, their Lord, the human being Jesus of Nazareth. It is he to whom they must now turn, whom they must now hear, obey, and follow. Although they know about the resurrected one, all they see before them is the human being, the suffering human being on his way to the cross. It is he whom they must believe, hear, follow. They are thrown back onto the path of suffering. They now travel that path with greater assurance; they can now travel it in faith because they know about the resurrection. At the present, however, they are still living in the world of the cross, not in that of the resurrected Lord. Here they must *hear, believe, follow.*

7. What happened there remained a mystery until the day of the resurrection. Although it was a comforting mystery for those who had to go along to Gethsemane, and into suffering, even their faith collapsed. They forgot the vision on Mount Tabor when they saw Jesus' shame on Golgotha. Faith collapsed. But the day of the resurrection came, and their faith was restored. In the resurrected one they now recognized the crucified one, and in the crucified the resurrected. Now we recognize in God the human being Jesus, whom we are to hear and to follow, and in the human being Jesus we recognize the Son of God who wants us to see his glory.

Sermon outline
Finkenwalde 1936

The Path of God

Luke 4:5–8: Then the devil led him up a high mountain and showed him in an instant all the kingdoms of the world. And the devil said to him, "To you I will give their glory and all this authority; for it has been given over to me, and I give it to anyone I please. If you, then, will worship me, it will all be yours." Jesus answered him, "It is written, 'Worship the Lord your God, and serve only him.'"

We have again come to Passiontide, and again we must collect our thoughts that we may understand what it means. Christ on the cross—that was the proclamation with which Paul set out. That was his God. That was the God for whom the first martyrs died. It was the God whom Luther rediscovered. And it is the same God whom we today are about to understand anew; or better, the same God who seizes us today anew. Christ on the cross, Christ the hidden king of the hidden kingdom—that is the message of the Protestant Church. Christ the revealed king of a visible kingdom—that is the message of the Catholic Church. Hence it is important that we understand what Passiontide is about. The time of Christ's passion begins not just in Passion Week, but on the first day of his preaching. He renounced the kingdom as a kingdom of this world not just on Golgotha, but from the very outset. These are the ideas expressed in our story. Jesus could have become the lord of the world. As the Messiah of Jewish dreams, he could have liberated Israel and led it to glory and honor. His entry procession could have been that of the visible king of this world. What a remarkable man this was, a man to whom dominion over this world is offered even before he begins his own work. And he is all the more remarkable in that he rejects the offer. So it is simply true, and not just biblically intended, that Jesus could have become the most splendid and powerful of all the kings of this world. He would have been honored; he would have been believed had he then dared to say he was the Son of God. After all, even the Roman emperors were believed when they said it. The world really would have become Christian. It would have had Christ as its king. It would have had the one who had been expected so long. The one whose power extends over all the earth, who establishes a reign of peace on earth. So Jesus could have had all that. He realizes in this instant that now, high on a mountain, for a moment, he is gazing upon all the kingdoms of the world, knowing he could be their ruler. But he also knows that a price must be paid for such dominion, a price which he deems too high. Dominion would be his only at the cost of his obedience to God's will. He must bow before the devil, go down on his knees before him, worship him. And that means he would have become a slave, and would no longer be free. He would be a slave to his own ambition; a slave of those who want him so eagerly. But he remains the free Son of God, and recognizes the devil who is trying to enslave him. [. . .]

Jesus knows what that means. It means debasement, revilement, persecution. It means being misunderstood. It means hatred, death, the cross. And he chooses this way from the very outset. It is the way of obedience and the way of freedom, for it is the way of God. And for that reason it is also the way of love for human beings. Any other path—be it ever so pleasing to people—would be a way of hatred and of contempt toward human beings, for it would not be the way of God. And this is why here, then, Jesus rejects the devil. Because it is the way of God through the world, he chooses from the very outset the way to the cross. And we are going with him, as individuals and as the church.

We are the church beneath the cross, that is, in disguise. Yet here as well, all we can do is realize that our kingdom, too, is not of this world.

Devotional
Berlin, Technical University, Passiontide 1932

Passiontide

I am spending Passiontide here for the second time. There arises protest in me when I read references in letters [. . .] to my "suffering." To me this seems like a sacrilege. These things must not be dramatized. It is more than questionable to me that I am "suffering" more than you or even than most people today. Of course, much of what happens here [in prison] is disgusting, but where is that not the case? Maybe we used to take things too seriously and solemnly in this regard. In the past I have sometimes marveled at how silently Catholics pass over such things. Is that perhaps not the greater strength after all? Maybe they know better from their own history what suffering and martyrdom really are, and are thus silent with regard to petty burdens and hindrances. I believe, for example, that "suffering" definitely also includes physical suffering, genuine pain, etc. We are so quick to emphasize spiritual suffering; yet it is precisely this suffering of which Christ should have relieved us, and I find nothing of this in either the New Testament itself or in the accounts of ancient Christian martyrs. It makes an enormous difference, after all, whether the "church suffers" or whether this or that happens to one of its servants. I believe much must be corrected in this regard; indeed, I must confess that I am sometimes ashamed at how much we have spoken about our own suffering. No, suffering must be something completely different, it must have a completely different dimension than what I have experienced thus far.

Dietrich Bonhoeffer to Eberhard Bethge
Tegel prison (Berlin), March 9, 1944

Discipleship
and the Cross

Mark 8:31–38: Then he began to teach them that the Son of Man must undergo great suffering, and be rejected by the elders, the chief priests, and the scribes, and be killed, and after three days rise again. He said all this quite openly. And Peter took him aside and began to rebuke him. But turning and looking at his disciples he rebuked Peter and said, "Get behind me, Satan! For you are setting your mind not on divine things but on human things." He called the crowd with his disciples, and said to them, "If any want to become my followers, let them deny themselves and take up their cross and follow me. For those who want to save their life will lose it, and those who lose their life for my sake, and for the sake of the gospel, will save it. For what will it profit them to gain the whole world and forfeit their life? Indeed, what can they give in return for their life? Those who are ashamed of me and of my words in this adulterous and sinful generation, of them the Son of Man will also be ashamed when he comes in the glory of his Father with the holy angels."

The call to discipleship occurs here in connection with Jesus' announcement of suffering. Jesus Christ must suffer and be rejected. It is the "must" of God's own promise, so that scripture might be fulfilled. Suffering and rejection are not the same thing. Jesus could, after all, yet be the celebrated Christ in suffering. The entire sympathy and admiration of the world could, after all, yet be directed toward that suffering. Suffering, as tragic suffering, could yet bear within itself its own value, its own honor, its own dignity. Jesus, however, is the Christ who is rejected in suffering. Rejection robs suffering of any dignity or honor. It is to be suffering void of honor. Suffering and rejection are the summary expression of Jesus' cross. Death on the cross means to suffer and to die as someone rejected and expelled. Jesus must suffer and be rejected by virtue of divine necessity. Any attempt at thwarting the necessary is satanic, even or precisely where such attempts come from the circle of disciples, for it is intent upon not letting Christ be Christ. That it is Peter, the rock of the church, who incurs guilt here immediately after his own confession to Jesus Christ and after his appointment by Jesus,[1] means that from its very inception the church itself has taken offense at the suffering Christ. It neither wants such a Lord nor does it, as the Church of Christ, want its Lord to force upon it the law of suffering. Peter's objection is his unwillingness to accept such suffering. With that, Satan has crept into the church. He wants to tear it away from the cross of its Lord.

This makes it necessary for Jesus to relate clearly and unequivocally to his own disciples the "must" of suffering. Just as Christ is Christ only in suffering and rejection, so also they are his disciples only in suffering and rejection, in being crucified along with Christ.[2] Discipleship as commitment to the person of Jesus Christ places the disciple under the law of Christ, that is, under the cross.

The mediation of this inalienable truth to the disciples, however, begins, strangely enough, with Jesus once again giving his disciples complete freedom. Jesus says: "*If* any want to become my followers."[3] That is to say, this is not self-evident even among the disciples themselves. No one can be coerced, nor can it even be expected of anyone; rather: "If any," despite all the other offers made to you, still want to become my followers. . . . So once again, everything depends on one's decision. Within the discipleship in which the disciples are standing, everything is as before broken off, everything is as before left open, nothing is expected, nothing coerced—so decisive is what is now to be said. So once more, before the law of discipleship is proclaimed, even the disciples themselves must be released from their commitment.

"If any want to become my followers, let them deny themselves." Just as in denying Christ Peter said, "I do not know the man,"[4] so also should each disciple say this to herself or himself. Self-denial can never be defined as some profusion—be it ever so great—of individual acts of self-torment or of asceticism. It is not suicide, since there, too, a person's self-will can yet assert itself. Self-denial means knowing only Christ, and no longer oneself. It means seeing only Christ, who goes ahead of us, and no longer the path that is too difficult for us. Again, self-denial is saying only: He goes ahead of us; hold fast to him.

". . . and take up their cross." In his compassion, Jesus has prepared his disciples for this statement by speaking first of self-denial. Only if we have genuinely, completely forgotten ourselves, such that we no longer know ourselves, can we be prepared to bear the cross for his sake. If we know only him, then we no longer know the pain of our own cross, as we are seeing only him. If Jesus had not prepared us so amicably for this statement, we could not bear it. As it is, however, he has enabled us to perceive even this harsh statement as a blessing. We encounter it in the joy of discipleship, and draw strength from it.

The cross is not adversity, nor the harshness of fate, but suffering coming solely from our commitment to Jesus Christ. The suffering of the cross is not fortuitous, but necessary. The cross is not the suffering tied to natural existence, but the suffering tied to being Christians. The cross is never simply a matter of suffering, but a matter of suffering and rejection, and even, strictly speaking, rejection for the sake of Jesus Christ, not for the sake of some other arbitrary behavior or confession. A form of Christian life that no longer took discipleship seriously, that made of the gospel merely a belief in cheap consolation, and for the rest did not really distinguish between natural existence and Christian existence—such a form of life had to understand the cross merely as one's daily trouble, as the distress and anxiety of our natural life. Here it was forgotten that the cross always simultaneously means rejection, and that the disgrace of suffering is part of the cross. Being expelled, despised, and abandoned by people in one's suffering, as we find in the unending lament of the psalmist,[5] is an essential feature of the suffering of the cross, yet one no longer comprehensible to a form of Christian life unable to distinguish between bourgeois and Christian existence. The cross means suffering with Christ, it means the suffering of Christ. Only that particular commitment to Christ occurring in discipleship stands seriously under the cross.

". . . and take up their cross." That cross is already there, ready, from the very beginning; we need only take it up. But to keep us from believing that we must simply choose any arbitrary cross, or simply pick out our suffering as we will, Jesus emphasizes that each of us has his or her *own* cross, ready, appointed, and appropriately measured by God. Each of us is to bear the measure of suffering and rejection specifically appointed for us. And the measure is different for each of us. God deems some worthy of great suffering, and to them he grants the blessing of martyrdom. Others he does not allow to be tempted beyond their strength. But still, it is the *one* cross.

It is laid upon every Christian. The first suffering of Christ we must experience is the call sundering our ties to this world. This is the death of the old human being in the encounter with Jesus Christ. Whoever enters discipleship enters Jesus' death, and puts his or her own life into death; this has been so from the beginning. The cross is not the horrible end of a pious, happy life, but stands rather at the beginning of community with Jesus Christ. Every call of Christ leads to death. Whether with the first disciples we leave home and occupation in order to follow him, or whether with Luther we leave the monastery to enter a secular profession, in either case, the one death awaits us, namely, death in Jesus Christ, the dying away of our old form of being human in Jesus' call. Because Jesus' call to the rich young man brings that man's death, because only as one who has died to his own will can he follow Jesus, because Jesus' commandment always means that we must die with all our wishes and all our desires, and because we cannot want our own death—for all these reasons, Jesus Christ in his word must be our death and our life. The call to discipleship, or baptism in the name of Jesus Christ, means death and life. Christ's call, or baptism, means placing the Christian into a daily struggle against sin and the devil. Hence every new day, with its temptations through flesh and the world, brings new sufferings of Jesus Christ upon his disciples. The wounds that are struck here, and the scars every Christian receives from this struggle, are living signs of the community of the cross with Jesus. But there is yet another suffering and yet another disgrace that no Christian escapes. Only Christ's own suffering is the suffering of reconciliation. Yet because Christ did suffer for the sake of the world's sins, because the entire burden of sin fell upon him, and because Jesus Christ bequeaths to the disciples the fruit of his suffering—because of all this, temptation and sin also fall upon the disciples. It covers them with pure shame, and expels them from the gates of the city like the scapegoat.[6] Thus does the Christian come to bear sin and guilt for others. Individual Christians would collapse under the weight of this, were they not themselves borne by him who bore all sins. In this way, however, they can, in the power of Christ's own suffering, overcome all the sins that fall upon them by forgiving them. Thus do Christians become the bearers of burdens: "Bear one another's burdens, and in this way you will fulfill the law of Christ" (Gal. 6:2). Just as Christ bears our burdens, so also are we to bear the burdens of our brothers and sisters. The law of Christ which must be fulfilled is the bearing of the cross. The burden of my brother or sister that I am to bear is not only that person's external fate, that person's character and personality, but is in a very real sense that person's sin. I cannot bear it except by forgiving it, in the power of the cross of Christ in which I, too, have a portion. Hence Jesus' call to bear the cross places every disciple into the community of the forgiveness of sins.[7] The forgiveness of sins is implied in the sufferings of Christ commanded to the disciples; it is imposed on all Christians.

But how is a disciple to know which is his or her cross? We receive it upon entering the discipleship of the suffering Lord, and come to recognize it in the community of Jesus.

Thus does suffering come to be the mark of the disciples of Christ. The disciple is not above the teacher.[8] Discipleship is *passio passiva*, having to suffer.[9] Thus did Luther count suffering among the signs of the real church.[10] Thus did an outline of the Augsburg Confession define the church as the community of those "who are persecuted and martyred for the gospel."[11] Those who are not prepared to take up the cross, those who are not prepared to give their life to suffering and rejection by others, lose community with Christ, and are not disciples. But those who lose their life in discipleship, in bearing the cross, will find it again in discipleship itself, in the community of the cross with Christ. The opposite of discipleship is to be ashamed of Christ, of the cross, and to take offense at the cross.

Discipleship is commitment to the suffering Christ. This is why the suffering of Christians is nothing disconcerting. Rather, it is pure blessing and joy. The accounts of the church's first martyrs attest that Christ transfigures the moment of highest suffering through the indescribable assurance of his proximity and fellowship. Thus, amid the most horrific torment which they bore for the sake of their Lord, they received the most extreme joy and blessedness of his community. The bearing of the cross proved to be the only way of overcoming suffering. But this applies to everyone who follows Christ, since it applied to Christ himself.

"And going a little farther, he threw himself on the ground and prayed, 'My Father, if it is possible, let this cup pass from me; yet not what I want but what you want' . . . Again he went away for the second time and prayed, 'My Father, if this cannot pass unless I drink it, your will be done'" (Matt. 26:39, 42).

Jesus asks the Father that the cup pass from him, and the Father answers his Son's prayer. The cup of suffering will indeed pass by Jesus, but *only insofar as it is drunk.* When he kneels for the second time in Gethsemane, Jesus knows that suffering will pass by insofar as he undergoes it. Only by bearing suffering will he overcome and conquer it. His cross is the overcoming of suffering.

Suffering is distance from God. Hence whoever stands in community with God cannot suffer. Jesus affirmed this Old Testament statement.[12] And for precisely this reason, he takes the suffering of the entire world upon himself and overcomes it. He bears the entire scope of this distance from God. Precisely insofar as Jesus drinks the cup, it passes by. Because Jesus wants to overcome the suffering of the world, he must drink of the cup completely. Hence suffering does indeed remain distance from God, but in the communion of the suffering of Jesus Christ, suffering is overcome through suffering, and community with God is bestowed precisely in suffering.

Suffering must be borne that it may pass by. Either the world itself must bear it and come to ruin through it, or it falls on Christ, and is overcome in him. Thus does Christ suffer vicariously in the place of the world. His suffering alone is redemptive suffering. But the community of faith, too, now realizes that the suffering of the world is seeking a bearer. Hence in the discipleship of Christ, suffering falls on that community of faith, and it bears that suffering by itself being borne by Christ. By following under the cross the congregation of Jesus Christ represents the world before God.

God is a God of bearing, enduring. The Son of God bore our flesh, and for that reason bore the cross. He bore all our sins, and through his bearing brought about reconciliation. Thus are his disciples also called to bear. Being Christian consists in bearing. Just as Christ preserves community with the Father through such bearing, so also is the bearing of his disciples community with Christ. Although one can certainly shake off the burden with which one is entrusted, doing so by no means completely frees one of that burden. A much heavier, more unbearable burden is now imposed, namely, the self-chosen yoke of one's self. All who suffer and carry heavy burdens are called by Jesus to cast off their yoke and take up his, which is easy, and to bear his burden, which is light.[13] His yoke and his burden are the cross. Walking under this cross is not misery and despair, but refreshment and peace for one's soul; it is the highest joy. Here we no longer walk beneath our self-made laws and burdens, but rather under the yoke of him who knows us and who himself walks along with us under this yoke. Under his yoke, we are assured of his proximity and fellowship. When a disciple picks up his or her own cross, it is actually Christ himself who is thereby found.

"Things must happen not according to your own knowledge, but rather above your own knowledge; immerse yourself in the abandonment of understanding, and I will give you my understanding. Abandonment of understanding is real understanding; not knowing where you are going is the right way to know where you are going. My knowing makes you completely unknowing. Thus did Abraham depart from his home without knowing whither. He surrendered himself to my knowledge and let go of his own knowledge, and travelled the right path to the right end. Behold, that is the way of the cross; you cannot find it, I must rather lead you like a blind person. Hence it is not you, nor any human being, nor any creature, but rather I, I myself, who will instruct you through my Spirit and word concerning the path you must stick to. Not the work you choose for yourself, not the suffering you think up for yourself,

but what comes to you quite contrary to your choosing, thinking, desiring, that is where you must follow, there I am calling,
there you must be a pupil, there it is high time, your teacher has
come" (Luther).[14]

Chapter in Part I of [The Cost of] *Discipleship*
London/Finkenwalde 1935/1936

Good Friday

Good Friday and Easter—the days of God's overpowering acts in history, acts in which God's judgment and grace were revealed to all the world—are just around the corner. Judgment in those hours in which Jesus Christ, our Lord, hung on the cross; grace in that hour in which death was swallowed up in victory. It was not human beings who accomplished anything here; no, God alone did it. He came to human beings in infinite love. He judged what is human. And he granted grace beyond any merit.

From a sermon on Romans 11:6
Barcelona, March 11, 1928 (Third Sunday in Lent)

Worldliness

Jesus Christ, the crucified reconcilor. First of all, this means that the whole world became god-less, without God, by rejecting Jesus Christ, and that by no effort of its own can the world remove this curse. The worldliness of the world received its signature once and for all through the cross of Christ. Yet because the cross of Christ is the cross of the world's reconciliation with God, that godless world simultaneously stands under the signature of reconciliation as God's free act. The cross of reconciliation means freedom to live before God in the midst of the godless world, that is, in genuine worldliness. The proclamation of the cross of reconciliation means liberation because it leaves behind those futile attempts to deify the world, proclaiming that the divisions, tensions, and conflicts between what is "Christian" and what is "worldly" are overcome, and summoning us to act and to live wholeheartedly in faith in this reconciliation between the world and God. Only through the proclamation of the crucified Christ can there be life in true worldliness, that is, neither in a way contradictory to the proclamation nor simply alongside it, based on some supposed autonomy of worldly things. Rather, it is precisely "in, with, and under" the proclamation of Christ that genuine worldly life is both possible and real. *Without or against* the proclamation of the cross of Christ, there is no realization that the world is god-less, without God, and has been left to itself by God. Rather, what is worldly will always try to satisfy its unquenchable longing for deification. And wherever the worldly establishes its own law *alongside* the proclamation of Christ, it completely falls prey to itself, and ultimately will put itself in God's place. In either case, what is worldly ceases to be worldly. Thrown back on itself, the worldly neither wishes nor is able to be merely worldly, and instead searches convulsively and despairingly for a deification of what is worldly. The result is that precisely this emphatically and exclusively worldly life deteriorates into false halfhearted worldliness. It lacks the freedom and courage to be genuinely, completely wordly, and is unable to let the world be what in reality it is before God, namely, a world that has been reconciled to God in its own godlessness. Only on the basis of the proclamation of the cross of Jesus Christ can there be genuine worldliness.

From: "God's Commandment in the Church," in *Ethics*
Berlin 1943

God's Love for Human Beings

The peace of Jesus Christ is the cross. The cross, however, is God's sword on this earth. It creates disunion. Son against father, daughter against mother, housemates against the head of the house, and all for the sake of God's kingdom and his peace—that is Christ's work on earth. Is it surprising that the world finds him guilty of hatred toward human beings, him who brought God's love to human beings? Who, then, is apt to speak thus about the love of father or mother, about loving one's son or daughter, if not either the destroyer of all life or the creator of a new life? Who can lay such exclusive claim to the love and sacrifice of human beings other than either the misanthrope or the savior of human beings? Who will carry the sword into the houses other than the devil or Christ, the Prince of Peace? God's love of human beings on the one hand, and human beings' love of their own kind on the other, are much too dissimilar. God's love of human beings means cross and discipleship, and yet precisely as such it means life and resurrection. "Those who lose their life for my sake will find it" (Matt. 10:39). This assurance is given by him who has power over death, the Son of God who goes to the cross and to resurrection and takes his followers with him.

From: "The Messengers. Exegesis of Matthew 10," in [The Cost of]
    Discipleship
Finkenwalde 1936/1937

Truthfulness

The truthfulness Jesus demands of his disciples is self-denial that does not conceal sin. Everything is visible and clear.

Precisely because truthfulness is concerned first and last with uncovering human beings in the entirety of their being, in their iniquity before God, it provokes the opposition of sinners, and is thus persecuted and crucified. The only basis of the disciples' truthfulness is that Jesus, while we follow him, reveals our sinfulness to us on the cross. The cross as God's truth over us is the only thing that makes us truthful. Whoever knows the cross no longer shies away from any other truth. Whoever lives under the cross is no longer subject to the law of establishing truthfulness by oath, for such a person stands in the perfect truth of God.

There can be no truth toward Jesus without truth toward human beings.

From: "The Sermon on the Mount. Matthew 5," in [The Cost of] *Discipleship*
Preliminary version: London 1934/1935
Final version: Finkenwalde 1936/1937

Suffering in Solidarity

It must be clear to us that most people learn only through personal experience occurring to their own bodies. *First,* this explains why most people are remarkably incapable of any sort of preventative action. We keep thinking that we ourselves will be spared when disaster strikes—until it is too late. *Second,* it explains our insensitivity toward the suffering of others; solidarity with suffering arises in proportion to our own increasing fear of imminent doom. Much can be said to justify this attitude. Ethically, we wish to avoid meddling with fate. We draw the inner calling and strength for action only from an actual and present crisis. We are not responsible for all the injustice and suffering in the world, nor do we wish to judge the whole world. Psychologically, our lack of imagination, sensitivity, and inner readiness is balanced by a kind of unwavering calmness, an undisturbed ability to work, and a great capacity for suffering. From a Christian perspective, though, none of these justifications can conceal that the real issue here is our hearts' lack of magnanimity. Christ avoided suffering until his hour had come; then, however, he went to it in freedom, seized it, and overcame it. Christ—so scripture tells us—experienced all the suffering of all human beings on his own body and as his own suffering (an incomprehensibly lofty notion!), and took it upon himself in freedom. We are certainly not Christ ourselves, nor are we called to redeem the world through our own actions and our own suffering, nor should we burden ourselves with the impossible and then castigate our own inability to bear it. No, we are not lords, we are instruments in the hand of the Lord of history. Only to an extremely limited degree are we really able to join with other human beings in suffering. Although we are not Christ, if we want to be Christians we must participate in Christ's own magnanimous heart by engaging in responsible action that seizes the hour in complete freedom, facing the danger. And we should do so in genuine solidarity with suffering flowing forth, not from fear, but from the liberating and redeeming love of Christ toward all who suffer. Inactive "waiting-and-seeing" or impassive "standing-by" are not Christian attitudes. Christians are prompted to action and suffering in solidarity not just by personal bodily experience, but by the experience incurred by their fellows for whose sake Christ himself suffered.

Notes from "After Ten Years"
Berlin, end of 1942

On Suffering

It is infinitely easier to suffer in obedience to a human order than in the freedom of one's own, personal, responsible deed. It is infinitely easier to suffer in company than alone. It is infinitely easier to suffer publicly and with honor than out of the public eye and in disgrace. It is infinitely easier to suffer through the engagement of one's physical being than through the Spirit. Christ suffered in freedom, alone, out of the public eye and in disgrace, in body and soul, and likewise subsequently many Christians along with him.

Notes from "After Ten Years"
Berlin, end of 1942

Limits

I find all this talk about human limits questionable. (Can even death, since people hardly fear it now, or sin, which people hardly even comprehend now, still be called genuine "limits"?) I always have the feeling we are merely fearfully trying to save room for God; I would rather speak of God at the center than at the limits, in strength rather than in weakness, and thus in human life and goodness rather than in death and guilt. As far as limits are concerned, I think it best simply to remain silent and to leave the unresolvable unresolved. The belief in resurrection is not the "solution" to the problem of death. The "beyond" of God is not the "beyond" of our cognitive capacity. Epistemological transcendence has nothing to do with God's transcendence. God is "beyond" our lives. The church is found not where human capacity fails, at the limits, but rather in the middle of the village. This is the sense of the Old Testament, and we still do not read the New Testament enough from the perspective of the Old Testament.

Dietrich Bonhoeffer to Eberhard Bethge
Tegel prison, April 30, 1944

Cain

Genesis 4:1: Now Adam knew his wife Eve, and she conceived and bore Cain.

Adam and Eve become the proud creators of new life, a new life which, however, is created in human beings' obsessive desire for life together and for death; Cain is the first human being born on the ground that is *cursed*. History begins with Cain, the history of death. Adam, preserved for death and yet consumed by a thirst for *life*, begets Cain, the *murderer*. The new element in Cain, Adam's son, is that he himself, in his being like God, violates human life. He who is not permitted to eat of the tree of life reaches all the more greedily for the fruit of death, the destruction of life. Only the Creator can destroy life. Cain usurps for himself the ultimate right of the Creator, and becomes a murderer. Why does Cain commit murder? Out of hatred toward God. This hatred is great. Cain is great. He is greater than Adam, since his hatred is greater, which means that his obsessive desire for life is greater. The history of death stands under the sign of Cain.

Christ on the cross, the murdered Son of God—that is the end of Cain's history, and thus the end of all history. It is the last, desperate assault on the gates of paradise. The human race dies under the slashing sword, under the cross. But Christ lives. The trunk of the cross becomes the wood of life, and in the middle of the world life is established anew in the accursed ground. In the center of the world, from the wood of the cross, the fountain of life springs up anew, and all those thirsting for life are called to this water, and whoever has eaten of the wood of this life will never again hunger or thirst.[1] A strange paradise, this hill of Golgotha, this cross, this blood, this broken body; a strange tree of life, this trunk on which God himself had to suffer and die— and yet here is bequeathed anew by God in grace: the kingdom of life, of resurrection, an open door of imperishable hope, of waiting, and of patience. Tree of life, cross of Christ, the center of God's fallen and preserved world, that is the end of the story of paradise for us.

> Today now he unlocks the door
> To blessed paradise.
> No angel bars it anymore,
> To God all honor, glory and praise.[2]

Text from a lecture series on Genesis 1—3 (and 4:1)
Berlin University, Winter Semester 1932/1933

Judas

Matthew 26:45b–50: "See, the hour is at hand, and the Son of Man is betrayed into the hands of sinners. Get up, let us be going. See, my betrayer is at hand." While he was still speaking, Judas, one of the twelve, arrived; with him was a large crowd with swords and clubs, from the chief priests and the elders of the people. Now the betrayer had given them a sign, saying, "The one I will kiss is the man; arrest him." At once he came up to Jesus and said, "Greetings, Rabbi!" and kissed him. Jesus said to him, "My friend, why have you come?" Then they came and laid hands on Jesus and arrested him.

Jesus had kept one mystery from his disciples until the Last Supper. Although he had not kept them in the dark concerning his path of suffering, and although he had even attested three times that the Son of Man must be delivered into the hands of sinners,[1] he had not yet revealed the deepest mystery. Not until the hour of ultimate community at the holy meal could he tell them that the Son of Man would be delivered into the hands of a sinner—through betrayal. One of you will betray me.[2]

His enemies cannot gain power over him alone. For that they need one of his friends, one of his closest friends who will deliver him over, a disciple who will betray him. This most horrible thing occurs not from without, but from within. Jesus' path to Golgotha begins with this disciple's betrayal. Some disciples sleep that incomprehensible sleep in Gethsemane,[3] one betrays him, and in the end "all the disciples deserted him and fled."[4]

The night of Gethsemane comes to completion. *"See, the hour is at hand"*—the hour Jesus had foretold, the hour about which the disciples had long known, the hour at whose arrival they quaked, the hour for which Jesus was so utterly prepared and the disciples so utterly unprepared, the hour that no worldly means could now delay any longer. "See, the hour is at hand, *and the Son of Man is betrayed into the hands of sinners."*

"Betrayed," Jesus says. It is not the world that gains power over him. Rather, Jesus is now delivered up, surrendered, abandoned by his own disciples. The protection they gave is now relinquished, they do not want to be burdened with him any longer: Let the others have him. And that is what happens. Jesus is discarded, his friends' protective hands fall to their sides. Let the hands of sinners do with him what they will. Let them seize him, those whose unholy hands were never permitted to touch him. Let them play with him, mock him, beat him. We can no longer do anything about it. That is what it means to betray Jesus: one no longer intervenes for him, one delivers him over to the mockery and power of the public, one lets the world do with him what it wants, one no longer stands by him. Jesus' own disciples deliver him over to the world. That is his death.

Jesus knows what is coming. Firmly and decisively, he summons his disciples: *"Get up, let us be going."* His menacing enemies had often had to retreat before him, he had walked freely through their midst, their hands had fallen.[5] At that time, his hour had not yet come. Now that hour is here. Now he goes to it freely. And to remove any doubt, to make it perfectly clear that the hour has come in which he will be betrayed, he says, *"See, my betrayer is at hand."* He does not even glance at the large crowd that approaches, at the swords and clubs of the enemy. They would have no power! Jesus' gaze falls only on him who has conjured up this hour of darkness. His disciples, too, are to learn where the enemy really is. For a single moment, everything—the history of salvation as well as world history—is in the hands of that one person: the betrayer. See, my betrayer is at hand—and with a shudder, in the night, the disciples recognize that person: Judas, the disciple, the brother, the friend. With a shudder—for when in the evening of that same night Jesus had told them "one of you will betray me," none had dared accuse the other. None could believe that the other could do this deed. So each asked, "Surely not I, Lord?"[6] One's own heart was sooner capable of such a deed than was the other person, one's brother.

"While he was still speaking, Judas, one of the twelve, arrived; with him was a large crowd with swords and clubs." We now see only the two persons who are really involved here. The disciples and sheriff's officers recede, all of whom are performing their own work poorly. Only two are performing their work the way they must: namely, Jesus and Judas. Who is Judas? That is the question, and it is one of the oldest, most brooding questions of the whole of Christianity. Let us stay initially with what the evangelist himself tells us: *Judas, one of the twelve.* Do we sense any of the horror with which the evangelist wrote this small sentence fragment?

Judas, one of the twelve—what more was to be said here? And did this not indeed say everything—the whole, dark secret of Judas, and at the same time the most profound horror at his deed? Judas, one of the twelve. But does this not mean it was simply impossible for this to happen; utterly impossible, and yet happen it did? No, there is nothing more to explain or comprehend here. It is utterly inexplicable and incomprehensible; it remains a complete mystery—and yet this deed happened. Judas, one of the twelve—this meant he was not only someone around Jesus day and night, someone who was a follower of Jesus, who had paid a price, who had left everything to be with Jesus, a brother, a friend, a confidant of Peter, of John, of the Lord himself. This meant something even more incomprehensible: Jesus himself had called and chosen Judas! That is the real mystery, for Jesus knew from the very beginning who would betray him. In the Gospel of John, Jesus says,

"Did I not choose you, the twelve? Yet one of you is a devil."[7] Judas, one of the twelve—here the reader is compelled to look not only at Judas, but with utter puzzlement at the Lord himself, who chose Judas. And those whom he chose he also loved. He let them participate in his whole life, in the mystery of his person, and likewise dispatched them to preach the gospel. He gave them the authority to exorcise the devil and to heal—and Judas was in their midst.[8] And nowhere is there any suggestion that Jesus secretly hated Judas. Quite the contrary, through his office as keeper of the disciples' purse Judas even seemed to have been distinguished from the others. It is true, John does once say that Judas was a thief,[9] but is this not actually a dark allusion to Judas having been a thief to Jesus, stealing from Jesus what was not his, and surrendering it to the world? And are not the thirty silver pieces actually a sign of how common and paltry are the gifts of the world for anyone who knows the gift of Jesus? And yet Jesus knew from the very outset who would betray him! Indeed, John even tells us of an utterly mysterious sign of intimacy between Jesus and Judas. The night of the Last Supper, Jesus extends to Judas the piece of bread dipped in the dish, and with this sign of utmost community, Satan enters into Judas. Jesus then speaks to Judas half as a plea, half as an order: "Do quickly what you are going to do."[10] No one else understood what was going on. Everything remained between Jesus and Judas.

Judas, one of the twelve, chosen by Jesus, accepted into community with Jesus, beloved—does this mean that Jesus is intent upon showing and proving his entire love even to his betrayer? Does it mean that he, too, is to know that, in fact, there is nothing to betray in Jesus? Does it also mean that Jesus loves God's will with the most profound love, a will coming to realization in his path of suffering, and that he also loves him whose betrayal opens the way, indeed, him who for a brief moment holds Jesus' fate in his hands? Does it mean that he loves him as the executor of the divine will, and yet knows: Woe to him through whom this comes about?[11] A great, unfathomable mystery: Judas, one of the twelve.

But this is also a mystery from the perspective of Judas himself. What does Judas want from Jesus? It must be that the evil one—the devil—cannot get away from him who is innocent and pure. He hates him, and yet because he cannot stay away from him, he also loves him with that same dark, passionate love with which the evil one is aware of his own origin in God, in the one who is pure. The evil one is intent upon being the disciple of the one who is good. The evil one is the most passionate disciple of the one who is good—until he betrays him. The evil one knows that he must serve God, and he loves God for the sake of God's power, a power he himself does not have. And yet he has but one urge: to gain power over God. Thus he is a disciple, and yet must betray his Lord. Jesus chooses Judas, and Judas cannot stay away from Jesus. Jesus and Judas belong together from the very beginning. Neither lets the other go.

And now we see this in the story itself: Jesus and Judas, linked by a kiss. Listen to the horrific: *"Now the betrayer had given them a sign, saying, 'The one I will kiss is the man; arrest him.' At once he came up to Jesus and said, 'Greetings, Rabbi!' and kissed him. Jesus said to him, 'My friend, why have you come?' Then they came and laid hands on Jesus and arrested him."* And, *"Judas, is it with a kiss that you are betraying the Son of Man?"* Again we are seized by the question: Who is this Judas who betrays the Son of Man with a kiss? A doubtless superficial answer is that the kiss was simply the usual form of greeting. This kiss was much more than that! This kiss was the completion of Judas's own path, the deepest expression of both the community and the abyssal separation between Jesus and Judas.

"My friend, why have you come?" Do you hear how Jesus still loves Judas, how even in this hour he yet calls him his friend? Jesus is not yet ready to let Judas go. He lets Judas kiss him. He

does not push him away. No, Judas must kiss him. His fellowship with Jesus must come to completion. Why have you come? Jesus knows why Judas has come, and yet: Why have you come? And, Judas, is it with a kiss that you are betraying the Son of Man? A final expression of a disciple's loyalty, coupled with betrayal. A final sign of passionate love, coupled with much more passionate hatred. Final enjoyment in a gesture of subservience, aware all the while of the superiority of his accomplished victory over Jesus. A profoundly contradictory act, this kiss of Judas! *Incapable of staying away from Christ, and yet to betray him.* Judas, is it with a kiss that you are betraying the Son of Man? Who is Judas? Should we here not also be mindful of the name he bore? "Judas." Does it not represent here the people itself from whom Jesus came, the deeply divided people, the chosen people that had received the promise of the Messiah and yet still rejected him? The people of Judah, who loved the Messiah and yet could not love him as he was? "Judas." His name actually means "thanks." Was this kiss not the thanks of the disciple's divided people offered up to Jesus, and yet at the same time an eternal renunciation?[12] Who is this Judas? Who is the betrayer? Faced with this question, are we capable of more than asking with the disciples: "Surely not I, Lord?"

"Then they came and laid hands on Jesus and arrested him." "It is I, I who should atone, bound hand and foot in hell. Scourge and bonds, what you have borne, my soul deserves."[13] Let us see how this ends! At the very hour Jesus completes his own redemptive suffering on the cross at Golgotha, Judas goes and hangs himself, condemning himself amid fruitless remorse.[14] Frightful community!

The whole of Christianity has always seen in Judas the dark mystery of divine rejection and eternal damnation. With horror it has acknowledged and witnessed God's seriousness and judgment upon the betrayer. For just this reason, however, it has never looked upon him with pride or arrogance, but rather has with trembling and acknowledgement of its own excessive sin sung the words: "O poor Judas, what have you done?"[15] And so today, too, let us say nothing more than precisely this: O poor Judas, what have you done? And let us take refuge in him who hung on the cross for the sins of us all and redeemed us; and pray:

> O Christ, God's Son, help us
> Through your bitter suffering
> That we, your servants always,
> All fault avoid.
> That your death and its cause
> We fruitfully remember.
> That, however poor and weak,
> Our thanks to you we give.[16] Amen.

Finkenwalde, Sermon on March 14, 1937 (Fifth Sunday in Lent)

Conversion

When we have completely renounced trying to make something of ourselves—be it a saint or a converted sinner or a cleric (a so-called "priestly figure"), a righteous or unrighteous person, a sick or healthy person (and all this I would call "the here and now," that is, living in the fullness of tasks, questions, successes, failures, experiences, and feelings of helplessness)—when we have done this, then we completely throw ourselves into God's arms, take God's own suffering in the world seriously rather than our own, and keep watch with Christ in Gethsemane. That, I think, is faith. That is conversion, and it is in this way that one becomes a human being, a Christian. How should we triumph because of success or despair because of failure if in this life, here and now, we suffer God's own suffering? You understand what I mean even if I say it with so few words. I am grateful that I have been permitted to realize this, and I know I could have done so only on the path I have indeed had to take. This is why I think with gratitude and peace of past and present things.

Dietrich Bonhoeffer to Eberhard Bethge
Tegel prison, July 21, 1944

Treasures
of Suffering

Romans 5:1–5: Therefore, since we are justified by faith, we have peace with God through our Lord Jesus Christ, through whom we have obtained access by faith to this grace in which we stand; and we boast in our hope of sharing the glory of God. And not only that, but we also boast in our sufferings, knowing that suffering produces patience, and patience produces experience, and experience produces hope, and hope does not disappoint us, because God's love has been poured into our hearts through the Holy Spirit that has been given to us.

"We have peace with God." So our struggle with God has now come to an end. Our recalcitrant heart has accommodated itself to God's will. Our own desires have become quiet. The victory is God's, and our flesh and blood, which hates God, is shattered and must be silent.

"Since we are justified by faith, we have peace with God." We see now that God is right. He alone. [. . .] God is righteous, whether we understand his ways or not. God is righteous, whether he punishes and chastises us or whether he pardons us. God is righteous, we are the transgressors. We do not see it, but our faith must confess it: God alone is righteous. Whoever thus acknowledges in faith that God alone is right in judging us, that person has come into the right position before God, has become rightly prepared to stand before God, has become righteous through faith in God's righteousness, and has found peace with God.

"We have peace with God through our Lord Jesus Christ." And so also has God's struggle against us been brought to an end. God hated the will that would not submit to him. Countless times he called, admonished, pleaded, and threatened, till there was no longer any patience in his wrath with us. He drew back and swung at us, and struck, struck the only innocent person on the entire face of the earth. It was his beloved Son, our Lord Jesus Christ. Jesus Christ died for us on the cross, struck down by God's wrath. God himself had sent him to this end. And God's wrath was stilled when his Son bent to his will and justice, even unto death. Miraculous mystery—God made peace with us through Jesus Christ.

"We have peace with God." Peace is found beneath the cross. Here one surrenders to God's will, here our own will comes to an end, here one finds repose and quiet in God, here one finds peace of conscience in the forgiveness of all our sins. Here beneath the cross one finds "access to this grace in which we stand," daily access to peace with God. Here is the only path in the world to peace with God. In Jesus Christ alone is God's wrath stilled and we ourselves are overcome and drawn into God's will. This is why the cross of Jesus Christ is for his congregation the eternal ground of joy in and hope for God's coming glory. "We boast in our hope of sharing the glory of God." Here in the cross God's justice and victory on earth have commenced. Here he will someday be revealed to all the world. The peace we receive here will become an eternal and glorious peace in the kingdom of God.

And yet though we would prefer to stop here, filled with the highest blessedness granted to us on this earth, namely, filled with the knowledge of God in Jesus Christ, with the peace of God in the cross—scripture here will not let us go. "And not only that . . . ," we now read. So not everything has been said so far. But what else is there to say after speaking of the cross of Jesus Christ, and of God's peace in Jesus Christ? Something must yet be said, something about you, about your life beneath the cross, about how God wants to test your life in God's peace so that this peace will be a reality instead of merely a word. Something must yet be said about your living yet a while on this earth, and about how you are to keep that peace.

That is why we now read: "And not only that, but we also boast in our sufferings." Whether we really have found God's peace will be shown by how we deal with the sufferings that will come upon us. There are many Christians who do indeed kneel before the cross of Jesus Christ, and yet reject and struggle against every tribulation in their own lives. They believe they love the cross of Christ, and yet they hate that cross in their own lives. And so in truth they hate the cross of Jesus Christ as well, and in truth despise that cross and try by any means possible to escape it. Those who acknowledge that they view suffering and tribulation in their own lives only as something hostile and evil can see from this very fact that they have not at all found peace with God. They have basically merely sought peace with the world, believing possibly that by means of the cross of Jesus Christ they might best come to terms with themselves and with all their questions, and thus find inner peace of the soul. They have used the cross, but not loved it. They have sought peace for their own sake. But when tribulation comes, that peace quickly flees them. It was not peace with God, for they hated the tribulation God sends.

Thus those who merely hate tribulation, renunciation, distress, defamation, imprisonment in their own lives, no matter how grandiosely they may otherwise speak about the cross, these people in reality hate the cross of Jesus and have not found peace with God. But those who love the cross of Jesus Christ, those who have genuinely found peace in it, now begin to love even the tribulations in their lives, and ultimately will be able to say with scripture: "We also boast in our sufferings."

Our own church has suffered much tribulation in recent

years. The destruction of its organization, the incursion of false proclamation, much hostility, angry words and defamations, imprisonment and distress of all sorts even up to this very hour—and no one knows what tribulations are still to come for the church.[1] But have we also understood that in all this God has wanted and yet wants to test us, and that in all this but one question is important—namely, whether we have peace with God or whether we have hitherto lived merely in an entirely worldly peace. How much grumbling and unwillingness, how much contradiction and hatred of suffering has come to light among us! How much denial, stepping aside, how much fear whenever the cross of Jesus began to cast even the tiniest shadow over our personal lives! How often have we believed ourselves capable of preserving our peace with God while simultaneously avoiding the suffering, renunciation, maliciousness, and threat to our existence! And the very worst is that we have had to hear repeatedly from our Christian brothers that they despise one another's suffering—and all because their own consciences would not leave them in peace.

But God will take no one into his kingdom whose faith has not proven genuine amid tribulation and suffering. "It is through many persecutions that we must enter the kingdom of God" [Acts 14:22]. This is why we must learn to cherish our tribulations before it is too late. Indeed, we must learn to rejoice in them and to boast of them.

But how? "Knowing that suffering produces patience, and patience produces experience, and experience produces hope, and hope does not disappoint us." Thus does God's word teach us how to view and understand tribulation correctly. The tribulation that seems so harsh and abhorrent in our lives is in truth full of the most wonderful treasures a Christian can find. It is like an oyster with a pearl inside, like a deep mine shaft in which one finds one metal after another the deeper one descends into it: first ore, then silver, and finally gold. Suffering produces patience, and then experience, and then hope. Whoever avoids suffering is throwing away God's greatest gifts along with it.

"Suffering produces patience." The Greek word for patience literally means to stay underneath, to endure, to bear rather than to cast off one's burden. Today we in the church know far too little about the unique blessing of enduring and bearing—to bear, not to cast off, to bear, but neither to collapse, to bear as Christ bore the cross, to endure beneath it, and there, underneath, to find Christ. When God imposes a burden, those who are patient bend their heads and believe it is good to be humbled thus—to endure *beneath* this burden. But to *endure* beneath it! To remain firm, to remain strong as well—that is what the word means, not anemic, giving in, shrinking back, enamored of suffering—but rather to gain strength under that burden as under God's grace, to preserve God's peace with unshakable constancy. God's peace is found among the patient.

"Patience produces experience." A Christian's life consists not in words, but in experience. No one is a Christian without experience. We are not talking here about life experience, but of the experience of God. But neither are we talking about all sorts of happenings which we connect with God, but about experiencing faith and God's peace as proving true, about the experience of the cross of Jesus Christ. Only the patient are experienced. The impatient experience nothing. Those to whom God wants to send such experience—an individual or a church—to them God also sends much temptation, uneasiness, and anxiety. They must cry out daily and hourly for God's peace. The experience about which we are speaking here leads us into the depths of hell and into the jaws of death and into the abyss of guilt and into the night of unbelief. Yet in all these things, it is not God's intention to take God's peace from us. In all these things we experience from day to day more of God's strength and victory, and the peace made at the cross of Christ.

That is why experience produces hope. For every temptation

that we experience as overcome is already the prelude to the final overcoming, and every conquered wave brings us closer to the land we yearn for. That is why hope increases with experience, and why in the experience of suffering there already dawns a reflection of eternal glory.

"And hope does not disappoint us." Where there is yet hope, there is no succumbing, and be there ever so much weakness, lament, and fearful crying—still, victory has already been grasped. That is the mystery of suffering in the church and in Christian life, that the very gate on which is written "abandon all hope," the gate of pain, of loss, of dying—that this very gate is to become for us the gate of great hope in God, the gate of honor and glory. "And hope does not disappoint us." Do we still have this great hope in God in and for our present church? If so, then all is won; if not, then all is lost.

"Tribulation produces patience, and patience produces experience, and experience produces hope, and hope does not disappoint us." But all this only for those who have found and who keep God's peace in Jesus Christ, and of whom our text now says: "God's love has been poured into our hearts through the Holy Spirit that has been given to us." Only those who are loved by God and who for that reason love God alone and above all else, those alone are permitted to speak thus. No, the gradation from tribulation to hope is no self-evident earthly truth. Luther said that one could very well put it quite differently, namely, that suffering produces impatience, and impatience produces obstinacy, and obstinacy produces despair, and despair disappoints us completely. Indeed, thus must it be if we lose God's peace, when we prefer an earthly peace with the world to peace with God, when we love the security of our lives more than we love God. Then must tribulation become our ruin.

But God's love has been poured into our hearts. Those whom God does through the Holy Spirit allow to experience that an incomprehensible thing is happening in them, namely, that they are beginning to love God for God's sake rather than for the sake of earthly goods and gifts, nor even for the sake of peace, but rather genuinely and only for God's own sake—those who have encountered God's love in the cross of Jesus Christ such that they begin to love God for the sake of Jesus Christ—those who through the Holy Spirit have been led to desire nothing more than to have a portion in God's love in eternity, and nothing other than this, absolutely nothing—they are saying from within this love of God, and with them the whole congregation of Jesus Christ: We have peace with God. We boast in our tribulations. God's love has been poured into our hearts.

Sermon at evening worship, March 9, 1938
Gross-Schlönwitz (Pomerania), Collective Pastorate

Disappointments

There are so many experiences and disappointments that drive sensitive people toward nihilism and resignation. That is why it is good to learn early that suffering and God are not contradictions, but rather a necessary unity. For me, the idea that it is really God who suffers has always been one of the most persuasive teachings of Christianity. I believe that God is closer to suffering than to happiness, and that finding God in this way brings peace and repose and a strong, courageous heart.

Dietrich Bonhoeffer to the Leibholz family
Zurich, May 21, 1942

Ecce Homo

"*Ecce homo*—behold, such a human being!" In him the world was reconciled with God. The world is overcome not through destruction, but through reconciliation. Not ideals, nor programs, nor conscience, nor duty, nor responsibility, nor virtue, but only God's perfect love can encounter reality and overcome it. Nor is it some universal idea of love, but rather the love of God in Jesus Christ, a love genuinely lived, that does this. This love of God for the world does not withdraw from reality into noble souls detached from the world, but experiences and suffers the reality of the world in the harshest possible fashion. The world takes out its rage on the body of Jesus Christ. But he, tormented, forgives the world its sins. Thus does reconciliation come about. Ecce homo.

The figure of the reconciler, of the divine human Jesus Christ, steps into the middle between God and world, into the center of all that happens. Through this figure, the mystery of the world is disclosed, just as in the same figure the mystery of God is revealed. No abyss of evil can hide from him through whom the world is reconciled with God. But the abyss of God's love encompasses even the most abysmal godlessness of the world. In an incomprehensible reversal of all righteous and pious thinking, God declares God's guilt toward the world and in so doing extinguishes the guilt of the world. God sets out upon the humiliating path of reconciliation and thereby pronounces the world free. God wills to be guilty of our sin, and takes over the punishment and suffering sin has brought upon us. God answers for godlessness, love for hatred, the saint for the sinner. Now there is no godlessness, no hatred, no sin which God has not carried, suffered, and atoned. Now there is no reality, no world that is not reconciled and in peace with God. God did this in his beloved Son Jesus Christ. Ecce homo!

Ecce homo—behold the incarnate God, the unfathomable mystery of God's love for the world. God loves human beings. God loves the world. God does not love some ideal person, but rather human beings just as we are, not some ideal world, but rather the real world. What we find disgusting in its opposition to God, what we evade, feeling pain and hostility, namely, the real human being, the real world—for God, this gives rise to un-fathomable love, it is something with which God intimately unites. God becomes a human being, a real human being. While we try to outgrow our being human, to leave the human being behind us, God becomes a human being, and we must recognize that God wants us, too, to be human beings, real human beings. While we distinguish between the pious and the godless, be-tween the good and the evil, the noble and the common, God loves real human beings without discriminating against any. God will not tolerate us dividing the world and human beings according to our own standards, and setting ourselves up as their judges. God leads us *ad absurdum* by becoming a real hu-man being, by becoming the companion of sinners, and by thus forcing us to become God's judges. God takes the side of real hu-man beings and of the real world against all their accusers. God accepts being accused along with human beings, along with the world, and in this way makes God's judges into the accused.

But it is not enough to say that God takes the side of human beings. This statement is based on one infinitely more profound, one whose meaning is much more impenetrable, namely, that in the conception and birth of Jesus Christ God physically took on humanity. God's love for human beings is put beyond any re-proach of inauthenticity, beyond any doubt and uncertainty by

God's entering into the life of human beings as a human being, by taking on and bearing the nature, essence, guilt, and suffering of human beings. For the love of human beings, God becomes a human being. He does not seek out and unite with the most perfect human being, but rather takes on human nature as it is. Jesus Christ is not the transfiguration of high humanity, but God's yes to real human beings. His is not the passionless yes of a judge, but the compassionate yes of one who suffers along with us. This yes contains the entire life and the entire hope of the world. In the human being Jesus Christ, judgment upon all humankind has been passed, though again not the indifferent sentence of the judge, but rather the compassionate judgment of him who has himself suffered through and borne the fate of all humanity. Jesus is not *a* human being, but rather *the* human being. Whatever happens to him also happens to human beings as such; it happens to everyone, and thus also to us. The name Jesus embraces all humanity and all of God.

The message of God's incarnation attacks at its very center an age in which the ultimate wisdom for both the evil and the good is either contempt for human beings or the idolization of human beings. The weaknesses of human nature reveal themselves more clearly in a storm than in the calm flow of peaceful times. In the face of unimagined threats and possibilities, it is anxiety, greed, dependency, and brutality that prove to be the prime movers of action for the vast majority. At such a time, the tyrannical despiser of human beings finds it easy to engage the baseness of human hearts by nourishing and renaming it. Anxiety is called responsibility, greed is called striving, dependency becomes solidarity, and brutality becomes lordship. Baseness is generated and multiplied ever anew in lascivious intercourse with human weakness. Amid the most sacred assertions of love for one's fellow human beings, the most base contempt for human beings plies its dark business. The more vulgar such baseness becomes, the more willing and pliable an instrument does it become in the hand of the tyrant. The tiny number of the upright is spattered with filth. Their courage is called rebellion, their discipline Pharisaism, their independence arbitrariness, and their lordship arrogance. The tyrannical despiser of human beings wants popularity to pass for a sign of the tyrant's great love for human beings, concealing the tyrant's secret, deep mistrust against all human beings behind the stolen words of genuine community. While the tyrannical despiser presents himself to the public as one of their own kind, he boasts of himself with the most repulsive conceit and disdains the rights of the individual. He considers people stupid, and they become stupid. He considers them weak, and they become weak. He considers them criminal, and they become criminal. His most sacred earnestness is a frivolous game, his bourgeois assurance of concern is the most insolent cynicism. Yet the more contemptuously he seeks the favor of those whom he despises, the more assuredly does he elicit the deification of his person by the crowds. Contempt for and idolization of human beings are intimate companions.[1] Good people, however—those who see through all this, and who withdraw from human beings in disgust, leaving them to themselves, those who would rather till their garden in seclusion than debase themselves in public life—these people succumb to the very same temptation of contempt as do those who are evil. Although their contempt for human beings is indeed more noble and sincere, it is also less productive, and less active. Their contempt can as little stand up before the incarnation of God as can tyrannical contempt. Whoever despises human beings is despising that which God loved, and, indeed, is despising the very form of the incarnate God.

There is also, however, a love for human beings that is intended to be sincere but that resembles contempt. It is based on an evaluation of human beings according to the values slumbering within them, according to their deepest soundness, reasonableness, and goodness. This love usually grows in times of calm, but even in times of great crisis the occasional flickering of these values can become the basis for a kind of well-intentioned struggle to bring oneself to love human beings. With coerced forbearance, evil is reinterpreted as good, baseness overlooked, the condemnable excused. For various reasons, one shies away from any unequivocal no, and ends up affirming everything. One loves a self-made image of human beings that hardly resembles reality, and thus in fact despises the real human beings whom God loved and whose nature God assumed.

God's incarnation alone makes it possible to know real human beings and not to despise them. Real human beings are permitted to live before God, and we are permitted to let them live alongside us before God without either despising or deifying them. Not because of some value that might be inherent in real human beings but only because God loved and was incarnate in the real human being. The ground of God's love for human beings resides only in God, not in human beings. And the ground permitting us to live as real human beings and to let real human beings live alongside us is likewise found only in God's incarnation, in God's unfathomable love for human beings.

Ecce homo—behold the *human being, judged by God,* a form of misery and pain. This is what the reconciler of the world looks like. The guilt of humanity has fallen upon him; it pushes him into disgrace and death under God's judgment. This is how costly reconciliation with the world is to God. Only by God executing judgment upon God can peace be established between God and the world and between human being and human being. The mystery of this judgment, however, of this suffering and dying, is God's love for the world, for human beings. What happened to Christ happened in him to all human beings. Only as someone judged by God can a human being live before God; only the crucified human being is at peace with God. In the form of the Crucified we recognize and find ourselves. Accepted by God, judged and reconciled in the cross: That is the reality of humankind.

In a world in which success is the measure and justification of all things, the form of him who was judged and crucified remains alien and at best pitiable. The world wants to and must be overcome through success. It is not ideas or attitudes, but deeds that decide. Success alone justifies past injustice. Guilt scars over in success. It is meaningless to reproach successful persons with their methods. This merely strands one in the past while the successful person strides forward from deed to deed, gains the future and makes the past irrevocable. Successful people create irreversible circumstances, what they destroy can never be rebuilt, what they build maintains the privilege of continued existence at least in the following generation. No accusation can make good the guilt through which the successful person proceeded. Accusation falls silent over time, while success remains and determines history. The judges of history play a pitiful role compared to those who shape history. History passes over them. No earthly power can dare claim as straightforwardly and as self-evidently as does history that the means justify the ends.

What has just been stated were facts, not value judgments. People and ages react in three different ways to these facts.

Wherever the figure of a successful person is most prominently on view, the majority succumbs to an *idolization of success.* It becomes blind to justice and injustice, truth and falsity, propriety and vulgarity. It sees only the deed, the success. The ability of ethical and intellectual judgment dulls before the glitter of success and before the desire to participate in some way in this success. One no longer even recognizes that guilt scars over in success precisely because guilt is no longer even recognized. Success is the utterly good, period. Only in a condition of intoxication is this attitude genuine and pardonable. In someone who has sobered up, it only comes at the price of profound inner falseness and conscious self-deception. The result is an inner depravity from which one can recover only with great difficulty.

The assertion that success is the good is countered by the assertion that focuses on the conditions of enduring success, namely, that only what is good will be successful. Here the ability of judgment is maintained over against success, here justice remains justice and offense remains offense. Here one does not close one's eyes at the decisive moment and then open them again after the deed is done. Here, too, one either consciously or unconsciously recognizes a law of the world according to which justice, truth, and order are in the long run more enduring than violence, falsity, and arbitrariness. And yet this optimistic thesis leads us astray. Either we must falsify the facts of history in order to demonstrate the failure of evil, in which case one quickly arrives at the opposite assertion that success is the good; or one's optimism falters in view of those facts so that we arrive at labeling all historical success heresy.

That all success comes from evil is then the eternal lament of the accusers of history. Mired in fruitless and Pharisaic criticism of the past, they never get to the present, to action, to success, and see in precisely this circumstance a confirmation of the wickedness of what is successful. Yet here, too, and without even knowing it, one makes success into the—albeit negative—measure of all things, and it makes no real difference whether success is the positive or negative measure of all things.

The form of the Crucified invalidates all thinking oriented toward success, for it is a denial of judgment. Neither the triumph of the successful nor the bitter hatred that those who have failed harbor against the successful will ever really get the better of the world. Jesus is certainly no advocate of the successful in history, but neither does he lead the rebellion of failed existences against the successful. He is concerned not with success or failure, but with his willing acceptance of God's judgment. Only in judgment is there reconciliation with God and among human beings. Christ counters all thinking focused on success and failure with the human being judged by God, be that human being successful or not. God judges human beings because it is out of pure love that God wants them preserved to stand before him. It is a judgment of grace that God brings upon human beings in Christ. In the cross of Christ, God shows the successful person the consecration of pain, of lowliness, of failure, of poverty, of loneliness, of despair. Not because all this might possess some inherent worth, but because it receives its sanctification through God's love, which takes all this upon itself as judgment. God's yes to the cross is judgment upon the successful. The unsuccessful, however, must realize that it is not their lack of success, not their status as pariahs[2] as such, but alone the acceptance of the judgment of divine love that allows them to stand before God. That it is then precisely the cross of Christ, and thus precisely the failure Christ incurs in the world, that again leads to historic success is a mystery of divine governance from which no "rule" can be derived, but which does repeat itself here and there in the suffering of his community.

It is only in the cross of Christ, and that means as those who are judged, that humankind attains its true form.

Ecce homo—behold the human being, accepted by God, judged by God, and awakened to a new life by God; behold the Resurrected! God's yes to human beings has found its goal through judgment and death. God's love for human beings was stronger than death. A new human being, a new life, a new creature has been created through God's miracle. "Life's is the victory, it has subdued death."[3] God's love became the death of death and the life of human beings. In Jesus Christ, the Incarnate, the Crucified and Resurrected, humankind became new again. What happened to Christ happened to everyone, for he was *the* human being. The new human being has been created.

The miracle of Christ's resurrection annuls the idolization of death regnant among us. Where death is the ultimate, fear of death is linked with stubbornness. Where death is the ultimate, earthly life is everything or nothing. Insistence on earthly eternities then belongs together with frivolous playing with life, and rigid affirmation of life belongs with indifferent contempt for life. Nothing betrays an idolization of death more clearly than when an age claims to be building for eternity and yet values human life as nothing, when one talks grandiosely about a new human being, a new world, a new society to be introduced, and yet all these "new" things consist in nothing other than an annihilation of present life. The radical nature of the yes and no to earthly life reveals that death alone counts for something. To grasp at everything or to discard everything: This is the posture of those who believe fanatically in death.

But where one recognizes that the power of death has been broken, where the miracle of the resurrection and of new life shines within the world of death, there one does not demand eternities from life; one accepts from life what it is able to give, not everything or nothing, but good things and bad things, the important and the unimportant, joy and pain. There one does not cling desperately to life, but neither does one throw it away thoughtlessly. There one is satisfied with the time allotted, and does not ascribe eternity to earthly things. One allows death to exercise the limited rights it does, after all, yet have. One expects the new human being and the new world, however, only from what is beyond death, from the power that has overcome death.

The resurrected Christ bears this new humanity within himself, God's ultimate, splendid yes to the new human being. Humanity does indeed yet live in the old, but is already beyond the old. It does indeed yet live in a world of death, but is already beyond death. It does indeed yet live in a world of sin, but is already beyond sin. The night has not yet ended, but the dawn has already begun.[4]

The human being accepted, judged, and awakened to new life by God: That is Jesus Christ, that is all humanity in him, that is we ourselves. The form of Jesus Christ alone is what encounters the world victoriously. This one form is the source of all formation brought about in a world reconciled with God.

The expression "formation" makes us suspicious. We have had enough of Christian programs, enough also of the thoughtless, superficial slogans of so-called practical Christianity instead of so-called dogmatic Christianity. We have seen that the formative powers in the world come from a quarter completely different from Christianity, and that so-called practical Christianity has failed in the world at least as much as has so-called dogmatic Christianity. We must thus understand by "formation" something quite different from that to which we are accustomed, and indeed, Holy Scripture does speak about formation in what is at first a completely alien sense for us. It is not concerned primarily with forming and shaping the world through planning and programs, but rather is concerned in every instance with one form only, namely, that form that has overcome the world[5]: the form and figure of Jesus Christ. Formation issues, only from this form, yet not such that Christ's teaching or so-called Christian principles are to be applied in any direct fashion to the world and the world shaped according to them. Formation comes about only by being drawn into the form and figure of Jesus Christ, *by being formed in accordance with the singular form and figure of the Incarnate, Crucified, and Resurrected.* This does not come about through exerting oneself "to become like Jesus," as we are used to saying, but rather by allowing the form of Jesus Christ to exert its own influence on us such that it shapes our form according to Christ's own (Gal 4:19). Christ remains the only one who forms and shapes. It is not Christians who form the world with their ideas, but rather it is Christ who shapes human beings into a likeness of his own form. But just as the form of Christ is misunderstood where Christ is understood essentially as the teacher of a good and pious life, so also would the formation of human beings be misunderstood if one were to see in it merely some sort of instruction for a good and pious life. Christ is the Incarnate, the Crucified and the Resurrected, just as Christian faith confesses.

To be transformed into his form[6] is the meaning of the formation of which the Bible speaks.

To be formed and shaped like the Incarnate: That is what it means to be truly human. The human being should and may be human. All efforts to be more than human, to be superhuman, all efforts to grow beyond one's humanity, all heroism, all attempts at being demigods are discarded here, for all of it is untrue. The real human being is neither an object of contempt nor of apotheosis, but rather of God's love. The multiplicity of God's creative wealth is not violated here by false uniformity, by coercion of human beings under an ideal, under a type, a particular image. Real human beings are allowed in freedom to be the creatures of their creator. Being formed in the image of the Incarnate means being permitted to be the human being one really is. There is no more pretense, hypocrisy, cramped coercion to be something other than what one is, something better, something more ideal. God loves real human beings. God became a real human being.

To be formed in the image of the Crucified means to be a human being judged by God. Such people carry with them in their daily lives God's death sentence, the necessity of dying before God for the sake of sin. With their lives they attest that nothing can stand before God except in judgment and in grace. Every day, they die the death of the sinner.[7] On body and soul they humbly bear the scars and stigmata inflicted by sin. There is no elevating oneself above anyone else, no setting oneself up as a model, for one knows one's self to be the greatest of all sinners. These people can excuse the sin of others, but never their own. All the suffering heaped upon them they bear knowing it serves to help them die to their own will and to acknowledge that God is right. Only by acknowledging that God is right both about and against them are they right before God. "Amid suffering the Master imprints his ever valid likeness into our hearts, our spirits."[8]

To be formed in the image of the Resurrected means to be a new person before God. Such people live in the middle of death, are justified in the middle of sin, and are new in the middle of what is old. Their secret remains hidden to the world. They live because Christ lives, and only in Christ. "For to me, living is Christ."[9] As long as Christ's glory is hidden, so also is the glory of their new life "hidden with Christ in God" (Col. 3:3). Those who know, however, already glimpse here and there what is coming. The new human beings live in the world, just like every other person, and often only a trifle distinguishes them from others. Nor are they concerned with singling themselves out, but rather only with singling out Christ for the sake of their fellows. Transfigured into the form of the Resurrected, here they bear only the sign of the cross and of judgment. By bearing it willingly, they show that they have received the Holy Spirit and have united with Jesus Christ in incomparable love and community.

The form of Jesus Christ acquires form in human beings. Human beings do not acquire any independent form of their own. What gives them form and shape and also preserves and maintains them in that new form is always and only the very form of Jesus Christ. So it is not just mimicry nor merely a repetition of his form, but rather his very form itself that acquires form in human beings. On the other hand, human beings are not transformed into some alien form, into God's form, but rather into a form of their own, the form belonging to their very essence. The human being becomes human because God became a human being. But the human being does not become God. It is thus not human beings themselves who were or are able to bring about this transformation of form; it is God himself who transforms his form into that of human beings. And he does this not so that human beings can be God, but rather so that they can be human before God.

In Christ the form of human beings before God was created anew. It was not a matter of place or time or climate or race or the individual or society or religion or taste—it was a matter of the life of humankind as such, of human beings recognizing here their image and their hope. What happened to Christ happened to humankind itself. It is a secret for which there is no explanation that only part of humankind recognizes the form and shape of its redeemer. To this very hour, the yearning of the Incarnate to acquire shape and form in all human beings does yet remain unfulfilled. He who bore the form of *the* human being can acquire form only in a small host, and that host is his church.

From "Ethics as Formation Power," in *Ethics*
Pomerania 1940

Christians
and Pagans

1. People go to God in their need,
   for help, happiness and bread they plead
   for deliverance from sickness, guilt and death.
   Thus do they all, Christians and pagans.
2. People go to God in God's need,
   find God poor, reviled, with neither shelter nor bread,
   see God entangled in sin, weakness, and death.
   Christians stand by God in God's suffering.
3. God comes to all human beings in need,
   sates them body and soul with His bread,
   dies the death of the cross for Christians and pagans,
   and forgives them both.

"Christians stand by God in God's suffering," and that distinguishes Christians from pagans. "Could you not keep awake with me one hour?" Jesus asks in Gethsemane. This is the reversal of everything a religious person expects from God. Human beings are called to suffer with God's own suffering caused by the godless world. That is, they must genuinely live in the godless world, and are not permitted to conceal or transfigure its godlessness in some religious fashion. They must live in a "worldly" fashion, and precisely in so doing participate in God's own suffering. They *are permitted* to live in a "worldly" fashion, that is, they are liberated from all false religious ties and hindrances. Being a Christian does not mean being religious in a certain way, or on the basis of some methodology to make something out of oneself, such as a sinner, penitent, or saint. It means being a human being. Christ creates us to be human, not to be some special type of human being. It is not some religious act that makes one a Christian, but taking part in God's own suffering amid worldly life. That is what conversion means: Not to think first of one's own distress or questions or sins or fears, but rather to allow oneself to be swept onto the path of Jesus Christ, into the messianic event itself, into the realization that Isaiah 53 is now fulfilled. Hence: "Believe in the gospel," or John's reference to the "Lamb of God, who bears the sin of the world" [. . .].

Being swept into the messianic suffering of God in Jesus Christ happens in the most varied ways in the New Testament: through Jesus' call to the twelve into discipleship; through the community of the table shared with sinners; through "conversion" in the narrower sense (Zacchaeus); through the actions of the woman who was a great sinner (though without any confession of sin; Luke 7); through the healing of the sick (see above [Isa. 53:4] Matt. 8:17); through accepting the children. Both the shepherds and the wise men stand before the manger not as "converted sinners," but simply because they—just as they are—are drawn to the manger (by the star). The centurion of Capernaum, who makes absolutely no confession of sin, is presented as an example of faith (cf. Jairus). Jesus "loves" the rich young man. The eunuch (Acts 8) and Cornelius (Acts 10) are anything but existences at the edge of the abyss. Nathaniel is "an Israelite in whom there is no deceit" (John 1:47), and finally there are also Joseph of Arimathea and the women at the tomb. The only thing these people have in common is having a share in God's suffering in Christ. That is their "faith." Not a word of religious methodology; the "religious act" is always something partial, while "faith" is something whole, an act of life. Jesus calls us not to a new religion, but to life.

Poem and Letter to Eberhard Bethge
Tegel prison, July 18, 1944

Hope

Christian hope in resurrection differs from that of mythology insofar as it directs us to life here on earth in a completely new and, compared to the Old Testament, even more incisive fashion. Unlike believers in the myths of redemption, Christians have no ultimate refuge from earthly tasks and problems in the eternal. Christians must partake of earthly life to the very end, just as did Christ ("My God, my God, why have you forsaken me?"), and only by doing so is the Crucified and Resurrected with them and are they themselves crucified and resurrected with Christ. This life here and now may not be prematurely suspended. This is the link between the Old and New Testaments. Myths of redemption arise from the human experience of limits, whereas Christ addresses us at the very center of our lives.

Dietrich Bonhoeffer to Eberhard Bethge
Tegel prison, June 27, 1944

The Beginning

The God of creation, of the utter beginning, is the God of the resurrection. From the very outset, the world stands under the auspices of Christ's resurrection from the dead. Indeed, precisely because we know about the resurrection we also know about God's creation in the beginning, about God's creation out of nothing. The dead Christ of Good Friday and the resurrected Lord of Easter Sunday: That is creation out of nothing, creation from the beginning. That Christ was indeed dead was not the possibility of his resurrection, but its impossibility; it was nothingness itself, the *nihil negativum*. There is absolutely no transition, no continuum between the dead Christ and the resurrected Christ other than God's own freedom to create in the beginning God's work out of nothing. If it were possible yet to intensify this *nihil negativum*, then here, concerning the resurrection, one would have to say that with Christ's death on the cross the *nihil negativum* broke its way into God's own being—"Oh, woe so great: God, God is dead"— and yet God, who is the beginning, lives, destroys the nothing, and creates the new creation in Christ's resurrection. It is through his resurrection that we know about creation, for if he were not resurrected, the Creator would be dead, and he would not bear witness to himself. From God's creation, on the other hand, we know about God's power to rise up again, we know God remains the Lord [over nonbeing].

From a lecture on Genesis 1:1–2
Berlin University, Winter Semester 1932/1933

Resurrection

The resurrection of Jesus Christ is God's yes to Christ and to his atoning work. The cross was the end, the death of the Son of God, curse and judgment upon all flesh. If the cross were the last word on Jesus, then the world would be lost in death and damnation without hope, and the world would have been victorious over God. But God, who alone effected salvation for us—"all this is from God" (2 Cor. 5:18)—raised Christ from the dead. That was the new beginning following the end as a miracle from above, though not like the springtime according to a fixed natural law, but rather according to the incomparable freedom and power of God that shatters death. "Scripture has proclaimed to us how one death devoured the other" (Luther).[1] Thus did God commit himself to Jesus Christ. Indeed, as the apostle is able to say, the resurrection is the day the Son of God is begotten (Acts 13:33; Rom. 1:4). The Son receives his eternal divine glory back, and the Father receives his Son back. Thus is Jesus confirmed and glorified as the Christ of God who Jesus was from the very beginning. But so also does God acknowledge and accept the vicariously representative, atoning work of Jesus Christ. On the cross, Jesus cried the cry of despair and then commended himself into the hands of his Father,[2] who was to make of both him and his work whatever he pleased. The resurrection of Christ confirms that God said yes to his Son and to his Son's work. And so do we now call upon the Resurrected as the Son of God, as Lord and as Savior.

The resurrection of Jesus Christ is God's yes to us. Christ died for our sins, and was resurrected for our righteousness (Rom. 4:25). Christ's death was the death sentence over us and our sins. If Christ had remained in death, this death sentence would still be in effect; "we would still be in our sins" (1 Cor. 15:17). But because Christ was raised from the dead, our own sentence has been repealed, and we have been resurrected with Christ (1 Cor. 15).[3] This is so because we are ourselves in Jesus Christ by virtue of God's acceptance of our human nature in the incarnation. What happens to him, happens to us, for he has accepted us. This is not a judgment from experience, but God's own judgment that seeks acknowledgment in faith in God's word.

The resurrection of Jesus Christ is God's yes to the creature. It is not a destruction of embodiedness, but rather the new creation of embodiedness that takes place here. The body of Jesus leaves the tomb, and the tomb is empty.[4] Just how it is possible or conceivable that the mortal, perishable body is now present as the immortal, imperishable, transfigured body[5] remains a mystery to us. Perhaps the different versions of the disciples' encounter with the Resurrected help to make clear that we ourselves are unable to imagine what is meant by this new bodiliness of the Resurrected. We do know that it is the same body—for the tomb is empty; and that it is a new body—for the tomb is empty. We do know that God has judged the first creation, and has created a new creation in the exact image of the first. It is not an idea of Christ that lives on, but the real, physical Christ. That is God's yes to the new creature in the midst of the old creature. From the resurrection we know that God has not abandoned the earth, but has reconquered it, has given it a new future, a new promise. The same earth that God created bore God's Son and his cross, and on this earth the Resurrected appeared to his disciples, and to this earth Christ will return on the last day. Whoever affirms Christ's resurrection in faith can no longer flee the world, but neither can they fall prey to the world, for in the midst of the old creation they have recognized God's new creation.

The resurrection of Jesus Christ demands faith. The one consistent witness of all these accounts, as divergent as they are in telling what occurred and was experienced here, is that the Resurrected appeared not to the world, but only to his followers (Acts 10:40f.). Jesus does not present himself to some impartial authority to attest before the world the miracle of his resurrection, thus coercing the world to acknowledge him. He wants to be believed, proclaimed, and believed again. The world, as it were, sees only the negative, the earthly impression of the divine miracle. It sees the empty tomb and explains it (albeit in conscious self-deception) as a pious deception on the part of the disciples (Matt. 28:11ff.). It sees the disciples' joy and message and declares it to be a vision or an auto-suggestion. The world sees the "signs," but does not believe the miracle. Only where the miracle is believed do the signs become divine signs and thus an aid to faith.

For the world, the empty tomb is an ambiguous historical fact. For believers, it is the historic sign—one following necessarily from and confirming the miracle of the resurrection—of the God who acts in history with human beings. There is no historical proof of the resurrection, only a plethora of facts that are extremely peculiar and difficult to interpret even for the historian. For example, we have the empty tomb. For if the tomb had not been empty, this strongest counter-argument against a physical resurrection would certainly have become the basis for anti-Christian polemic. Nowhere, however, do we encounter this objection. In fact, the opposing side confirms the empty tomb (Matt. 28:11). Or we have the sudden turn of events two days after the crucifixion. Any conscious deception is excluded psychologically by virtue of the disciples' entire earlier and subsequent behavior, and also by the divergent nature of the resurrection accounts themselves. Self-deception through visionary states is rendered virtually an impossibility for the unbiased historian, given the disciples' own initially quite unbelieving and skeptical rejection of the message (Luke 23:11 *et passim.*), together with the considerable number and the manner of appearances. Hence the historians' evaluation of this matter, which from a scientific perspective remains such a riddle, will be dictated by presuppositions contained in their worldview. But this robs their conclusions of any interest or import for faith, which is grounded in God's acts in history.

So for the world an insoluble riddle does remain, but not one that in and of itself could ever coerce belief in the resurrection of Jesus. For faith, however, this riddle is a sign of the reality about which it already knows, an imprint of divine activity within history. Research can neither prove nor disprove the resurrection of Jesus, for it is a miracle of God. Faith, however, to whom the Resurrected attests himself as the living Christ, recognizes precisely in the witness of scripture the historic nature of the resurrection as an act of God which in its miraculous nature can only be a riddle for science. Faith receives the certainty of the resurrection only from the present witness of Christ. It finds its confirmation in the historic imprints of the miracle as recounted by scripture.

It is the blessing of Jesus Christ that he does not yet reveal himself visibly to the world, for the very moment that happened would be the end and thus the judgment on unbelief. So the Resurrected withdraws from any visible salvaging of his honor before the world. In his hidden glory he is with his community, and is attested through the word before all the world, till at the Last Judgment he will come, visible to all human beings, to judge them all.

Theological Letter on "Easter"
    commissioned by the Pomeranian Council of Brethren
Berlin, March 1940

Easter

Easter? We focus more on dying than on death. How we deal with dying is more important to us than how we conquer death. [. . .] Learning to deal with dying, however, does not yet mean we have learned to deal with death. Overcoming dying occurs within the realm of human possibilities, while overcoming death means resurrection. It is not from the *ars moriendi,* but from the resurrection of Christ that a new, purifying breeze can blow into the present world. [. . .] If even a few people were really to believe this, allowing this belief to move them in their earthly actions, much would change. To live from the perspective of the resurrection: That is Easter.

Dietrich Bonhoeffer to Eberhard Bethge
Tegel prison, March 27, 1944

Resurrection
Instead of Immortality

1 Corinthians 15:17: If Christ has not been raised, your faith is futile
and you are still in your sins.

A dangerous text for Easter. For when we examine it closely,
and allow it to impress itself upon us, it may be that it robs us of
all our Easter joy, and thus it seems improper to speak of such
serious, dangerous things at Easter. And yet, among Christian
feast-days, there is not a single one that, if we take it seriously,
does not seem dangerous enough to cause fear and anxiety in
our hearts. Our entire existence and our entire spiritual being is
assaulted and brought to judgment, and called to decision. The
message of Christmas is no different in this regard than that of
Easter. Yet only if we undergo this assault ever anew and ever
more profoundly can we master it and sense something of genuine Easter joy, which is anything but sentimentality.

If Christ has not been raised, our faith is futile, and that means
we are still living in guilt before God, and means finally that we
are the most miserable human beings on earth. In other words,
if Christ has not been raised, then that which supports our lives
is removed, and everything collapses; our lives sink into meaninglessness. All talk of divine things is illusory, all hope is
ephemeral. Our lives depend on Easter, Paul tells us. What do
we say to this?

Beginning with childhood, each of us comes to view Easter
with joy, anticipating the coming spring, with all the happiness
the warm sun pours into our hearts, and we grow fond of that

celebration full of warm memories and do not wish to part with it. Who among us would be willing to give up even a single spring of our lives? But who among us would want or even be able to say that our entire life depends on this Easter celebration, and that our very existence would be threatened if there were no Easter? But Paul said this. And because he reflected upon this question a bit more thoroughly than we are wont to do, we might assume that his statement does harbor a certain meaning upon which we, too, might reflect with some profit. "If Christ has not been raised, your faith is futile."

Apparently everything depends on understanding correctly what Paul means by the word "raised." What does resurrection mean, and what can it mean for us? These are the traditional Easter questions which we must strive to answer. Otherwise we would have to admit to being thoughtless. It was the overwhelming fact of the perpetually self-renewing spring itself that gave people in all the world an intimation of some primal struggle between darkness and light, a struggle in which after hard fighting light does emerge victorious—spring emerges from the dark winter. Every year this enormous spectacle of nature renews itself and awakens in humankind an intimation of resurrection hope. All that is dark must ultimately become light. That is a law of nature. Indeed, darkness does not even really exist on its own; it consists merely in the absence of light; a single beam of sunlight annihilates it. And the sun does come, comes with absolute certainty, and with it the resurrection of nature. The death of nature already contains the germs of life. Death is not really death at all, but an epoch of life that in seminal form endures in seemingly rigid bodies. Life and light must be victorious, and death and darkness are merely modes of appearance of life and light. Such thoughts are the common and primal property of humankind reaching back into its most primitive spiritual life. To such thoughts our own, modernized Easter faith is reduced without our even noticing that Christianity has something quite different to say about Easter.

Easter does not celebrate a struggle between darkness and light that in any case must finally be won by light, since darkness is, in actual fact, nothing at all, and death is, after all, already life. It does not celebrate a struggle between winter and spring, between ice and sunshine. Rather, it remembers the struggle of guilty humankind against divine love, or better: of divine love against guilty humankind; a struggle in which God seems to succumb on Good Friday and in which precisely by succumbing he actually is victorious on Easter. Is God victorious, or is Prometheus victorious?[1] This is the question that at Easter is answered by God's mighty act. Good Friday is not the darkness that necessarily must give way to light. Nor is it the winter sleep or hibernation that stores and nurtures the germ of life. Rather, it is the day when the incarnate God, incarnate love, is killed by human beings who want to become gods themselves. It is the day when the Holy One of God, that is, God himself, dies, really dies—of his own will and yet as a result of human guilt, and no germ of life is spared in him such that his death might resemble sleep. Good Friday is not, like winter, a transitional stage. No, it really is the end, the end of guilty humankind and the final judgment humankind pronounces on itself. And here only one thing can help: God's mighty act coming from God's eternity and taking place among humankind. Easter is not an immanent, inner-worldly occurrence, but a transcendent one, and that means a more than worldly occurrence, God's intervention from within eternity and commitment to God's Holy One by raising him from the dead. Easter speaks not about immortality, but rather about resurrection, resurrection from death, death that really is death with all its terrors and horrors, a death of body and soul, of the whole person—resurrection through God's mighty act. That is the message of Easter. Easter speaks not about divine seeds inhering within human beings, seeds which as in nature again and again celebrate resurrection, but rather about human guilt, and about death, yet also about God's love and about the death of death, about God's eternal, mighty act—and not about immanent laws of nature.

If God's history among human beings had come to an end on Good Friday, the last word on humankind would be: guilt, revolt, unfettering of all human-titanic powers, storming of heaven by human beings, godlessness, abandonment by God, which ends up ultimately in meaninglessness and despair. "Then your faith is futile. Then you are still in your sins. Then we are the most miserable of all human beings." That is, the last word spoken is: humankind. On the cross of Jesus Christ, not only does our moral and religious life come to ruin by being found guilty, but our entire culture is also judged. If the cross had been the end, it would also have meant the end of science and art. All our cultural activity aims at something ultimate, at meaning, at a *logos,* at God. What sense does the search for truth make if there is no truth, if human beings rather than God are the ultimate standard for what is true and false? The vital nerve of our art is severed when art is robbed of this trajectory toward something ultimate, meaningful, divine. If God is dead—well, then we are the most miserable of human beings. We now understand this together with the apostle.

A rather strange story from antiquity relates how a small boat of Greek sailors sailed along the southern Italian coast, and how they suddenly heard a powerful, lamenting voice calling the name of the helmsman. When the helmsman answered, they heard the same voice cry: The great Pan is dead, the great Pan is dead! Great fear and panic spread over the ship, and wherever this news was heard, people fled in confusion and terror. Although this puzzling story has been variously interpreted, one thing seems certain to me: It is a pagan counter to the message of Good Friday—God is dead, the world is godless and abandoned by God. And people's terror and confusion express the horrified, terror-stricken question: What now? If God is dead, the world must go under, must collapse into meaninglessness.

The ancient world had no response to the great lament, "the great Pan is dead." The Christian message of Easter supplied the answer. The meaning of the *Easter* message is: God is the death of death, God lives, and so also does Christ live; death was not able to keep him against the superiority of God. God pronounced the mighty word against death, destroyed it, and raised Jesus Christ.

What does this mean? How are we to understand this? Countless questions come to mind. What about the notion of corporeal resurrection? The empty tomb? The appearances? A whole host of questions—curiosity, delight in superstitious things, mystery mongering, none of which can ever please us—questions rambling from one thing to another, never satisfied. Certainly the tomb was empty. The only important thing, however, is God's commitment to Christ, God's touching him with eternal life. Now Christ lives because God lives, and because God's love lives. That is enough for us. We can ponder the "how," but this will not change anything about the fact "that."

But if God lives, then so also does love live despite the cross. Then we no longer live in sin, and God has forgiven us. In unison with God's commitment to Jesus, Jesus committed himself to us. If Jesus lives, then our faith acquires new meaning. Then we are the most blessed of all people. God's "yes" to guilty humankind, new meaning for all our actions: That is Easter. Not "the great Pan is dead," but: God lives, and with him we as well. That is Easter. Not abandonment by God, but the fullness of God. Not humanity and its titanic victory over the deity, but God and God's mighty victory over humankind, over death and guilt and rebellion. That is Easter.

But one more thing. Very gently and discretely, a certain hope begins to sprout for us on Easter Sunday. "If for this life only we have hoped . . . ," Paul says.[2] Easter is God's intervention from within eternity, we said. Easter is the prelude to ultimate, inexpressible things that will come to pass when the consummation is near, things about which we can now speak only in metaphors and parables. It is not just today that Easter concerns us. No, it reveals to us the entire glory and power of God. God is the Lord of death, not only of Jesus Christ's death, but of yours and mine as well. Yet just as God raised Jesus with unutterable authority and power, so also will he lead his holy people out of death and to life. And it is to this that we look forward today in hope.

Sermon on Easter Sunday
Barcelona, April 8, 1928

Fate

The liberating thing about Good Friday and Easter is that one's thoughts are swept far beyond one's own personal fate to the ultimate meaning of all life and suffering, and of whatever occurs, such that one is seized by a great hope.

Dietrich Bonhoeffer to his family
Tegel prison, April 25, 1943 (Easter Sunday)

Incarnation— Cross—Resurrection

In Jesus Christ we believe in the incarnate, crucified, and resurrected God. In the incarnation we recognize God's love for God's creation, in the crucifixion God's judgment over all flesh, and in the resurrection God's will to a new world. Nothing would be more distorted than to tear these three pieces apart, since each contains the whole. As inappropriate as is any establishment of a theology of incarnation, of the cross, or of resurrection against the others by falsely viewing any one of these parts as absolute, just as false is such juxtaposition for a reflection on Christian life. Christian ethics based exclusively on the incarnation would too easily lead to a compromise solution. Ethics based exclusively on either the cross or the resurrection of Jesus Christ would fall prey to radicalism and rapturous enthusiasm. Only unity can resolve the conflict between the parts.

Jesus Christ, the human being: This means that God enters into created reality and that we may and should be human beings before God. The destruction of human existence is sin, and as such hinders God from redeeming human beings. Nevertheless, the existence of Jesus Christ as a human being does not simply represent a confirmation of the existing world and of human nature. Jesus was a human being "without sin" (Heb. 4[:15]); that is the decisive point. Among other human beings, however, Jesus lived in deep poverty, unmarried, and died as a criminal. So Jesus' human existence already contains a double condemnation of human beings: the absolute condemnation of sin and the relative condemnation of existing human circumstances.

With the inclusion of this double condemnation, however, Jesus is genuinely a human being, and wants us to be human beings as well. Without either declaring human reality autonomous or destroying it, he allows it to continue as something penultimate that in its own way needs to be taken both seriously and not seriously, as something penultimate that has become the outer covering of the ultimate.

Jesus Christ, the Crucified: This means that God has pronounced the final judgment over fallen creation. God's rejection which happened on the cross of Jesus Christ contains the rejection of the human race without exception. The cross of Jesus is the death sentence over the world. Here human beings cannot boast of their being human nor the world of its divine order. Here human glory has come to its final end in the image of the beaten, bleeding, spat-upon face of the Crucified. And yet the crucifixion of Jesus does not simply mean the annihilation of creation. Rather, it is under the symbol of death—the cross—that human beings are now to live on, in judgment upon themselves if they despise it, or toward their own salvation if they acknowledge it. The ultimate has become real in the cross as judgment upon all that is penultimate, and simultaneously as grace upon the penultimate that submits to the judgment of the ultimate.

Jesus Christ, the Resurrected: This means that out of love and omnipotence God brings death to an end, calls a new creation to life, bestows new life. "Everything old has passed away."[1] "See, I am making all things new."[2] Resurrection has already commenced in the midst of the old world as a final sign of its end and of its future, and simultaneously as living reality. Jesus was resurrected as a human being, and thus did he grant resurrection to human beings. And thus also do human beings remain human even though, being new and resurrected, they in no way resemble the old human beings. To be sure, however, up to the boundary of their own death, those who are already resurrected with

Christ remain in the world of the penultimate, the world into which Jesus himself entered and in which the cross stands. Thus as long as the earth exists, the resurrection will not suspend the penultimate, even though eternal life, new life breaks into earthly life ever more powerfully and creates space for itself in that life.

Incarnation, cross, and resurrection may have become clear now in both their unity and their difference. Christian life is life with the incarnate, crucified, and resurrected Jesus Christ, whose word encounters us as a whole in the message of the justification of the sinner through grace. Christian life means being human by virtue of the incarnation, it means being judged and pardoned by virtue of the cross, and means to live a new life in the power of the resurrection. None of these becomes real without the others.

From: "The Ultimate and Penultimate Things," in *Ethics*
Ettal Monastery (Bavaria), 1940

Tension

I have long been fond of the time between Easter and Ascension. After all, here, too, there is great tension. How are human beings to endure earthly tensions if they know nothing of the tension between heaven and earth?

Dietrich Bonhoeffer to Eberhard Bethge
Tegel prison, April 11, 1944

The Visible Community of Faith

Matthew 5:13–16: You are the salt of the earth; but if salt has lost its taste, how can its saltiness be restored? It is no longer good for anything, but is thrown out and trampled under foot. You are the light of the world. A city built on a hill cannot be hid. No one after lighting a lamp puts it under the bushel basket, but on the lampstand, and it gives light to all in the house. In the same way, let your light shine before others, so that they may see your good works and give glory to your Father in heaven.

The addressees here are those whom the Beatitudes called into the grace of discipleship of the Crucified. Those who were called blessed in the Beatitudes, while being considered worthy of the kingdom of heaven, obviously nevertheless appeared to be utterly unworthy of life on this earth,[1] or to be superfluous. Here, now, they are designated by the symbol of a substance which is indispensable for life on earth. They are the salt of the earth. They are the earth's most noble possession, its most precious asset. Without them, the earth cannot continue to live. The earth is kept alive by salt. For the sake of precisely these poor, ignoble, weak, whom the world rejects, the earth itself lives. It destroys its own life by expelling the disciples, and—a miracle!—precisely for the sake of these outcasts the earth is permitted to live on. This "divine salt" (Homer)[2] maintains its efficacy. Its effects permeate the whole earth. It is the earth's substance. Thus are the disciples not only directed toward the Kingdom of Heaven, but also reminded of their mission on earth. As those bound only to Jesus, they are directed to the earth, whose salt they are. By calling not himself, but his disciples the salt of the earth, Jesus assigns to them an activity on the earth. He draws them into his own work. He remains among the people of Israel while the disciples are commissioned to work on the entire earth.[3] Only insofar as that salt remains salt, and maintains its purifying, seasoning powers, can it maintain and preserve the earth. For its own sake as well as for the earth's sake, salt must remain salt, and the congregation of disciples must remain what through Christ's call it really is. Its activity on earth and its preserving power will consist in remaining true to its calling. Salt is supposed to be imperishable, and thereby an enduring power of purification. This is why the Old Testament uses salt in sacrifices, and why in the Catholic baptismal rite salt is put into the child's mouth (Ex. 30:35; Ezek. 16:4). The guarantee of the permanence of the community of faith resides in the imperishable quality of salt.

"You *are* the salt"—not: You should be the salt! It is not for the disciples to decide whether they are or are not to be salt. Nor is any appeal made to them to become the salt of the earth. They are that salt, whether they want to be or not, in the power of the call they have encountered. You *are* the salt—not: You have the salt. It would be an unwarranted abbreviation were one to follow the Reformers and equate the disciples' message with the salt.[4] What is meant is their entire existence insofar as it is grounded anew through Christ's call to discipleship, this existence of which the Beatitudes speak. Those who have been called by Jesus and stand in his discipleship are, through precisely that call, the salt of the earth in their entire existence.

The other possibility, however, is that the salt loses its taste, and ceases to be salt. Its activity ceases. And then, indeed, it is good for nothing except to be thrown away. That is the distinction of salt. Every thing must be salted. But salt that has lost its taste can never again be salted. Everything, even the most rotten stuff, can be saved by salt; only salt itself that has lost its taste is hopelessly ruined.[5] That is the other side. That is the threatening judgment hovering over the community of disciples. The earth is to be saved by the community of faith; only the congregation that ceases to be what it is is hopelessly lost. The call of Jesus means being the salt of the earth or being destroyed. Either follow in discipleship or the call itself will annihilate the person called. There is no second chance for being saved. There cannot be.

Along with Jesus' call, the congregation of disciples receives not only the invisible efficacy of salt, but also the visible radiance of light. "You *are* the light"—again, not: You should be the light. The call itself has made them into this. Nor can it be otherwise now; they are a light that is seen. If this were not so, the call itself apparently would not be with them. What an impossible, nonsensical goal it would be for Jesus' disciples, for *these* disciples, to want to *become* the light of the world! They have already been made such by the call itself, and within discipleship itself. And again, not: "You *have* the light," but "You are the light!" The light is not something given to you, for example, as your proclamation, but rather you yourselves are that light. The same one who says of himself in direct speech, "I am the light,"[6] says to his disciples in direct speech: You are the light in your entire lives insofar as you abide in my call. And because you are the light, you can no longer remain hidden, whether you want this or not. Light shines, and the city built on a hill cannot be hid. It cannot. It is visible from afar, either as a secure city or as a guarded citadel or as collapsed ruins. This city on the hill—what Israelite will not think of Jerusalem, the city built on high![7]—is the congregation of disciples itself. Those who follow are now no longer faced with any decision of this sort. The only decision relevant to them has already been made. They must now be what they are, or they are not followers of Jesus. Those who follow are the visible community of faith. Their act of following, of discipleship, is a visible activity singling them out from the world—or it is not discipleship. And this discipleship is as visible as light in the night, as a hill on the plain.

To flee into invisibility is to deny the call. A congregation of Jesus that seeks to be an invisible congregation is no longer a congregation of disciples. "No one after lighting a lamp puts it under the bushel basket, but on the lampstand." That is the other possibility, namely, that the call is denied by consciously concealing the light and extinguishing it under the bushel basket. This bushel basket under which the visible community of faith hides its light can be both fear of human beings and conscious accommodation to the world for whatever purpose—for missionary purposes or because of misunderstood love for human beings. But it may also—and this is even more dangerous—be a so-called reformational theology that even dares to call itself *theologia crucis*,[8] a theology which is characterized by a rejection of "Pharisaic" visibility for the sake of "humble" invisibility in the form of total accommodation to the world. The mark of the community of faith here is not that it is visible in some extraordinary form, but rather that it lives up to the *iustitia civilis*.[9] That the community's light *not* shine has here been made into the criterion of Christian existence. But Jesus says: Let your light shine before the Gentiles. In any event, it is the light of Jesus' call that shines here. What kind of light is this light in which these disciples of Jesus, the disciples of the Beatitudes, are to shine? What kind of light is to come from that particular place to which the disciples alone have a claim? Considering that the disciples stand beneath the invisible and hidden cross of Jesus, what does this have to do with the light that is to shine? Does not the very fact that the cross is hidden imply that the disciples, too, are to remain concealed rather than stand in the light? It is an evil bit of sophistry that concludes from the cross of Jesus that the church is to accommodate itself to the world. Would it not be clear to an unsophisticated listener that precisely there, on the cross, something extraordinary has become visible? Or is all this perhaps *iustitia civilis*, is the cross itself accommodation to the world? Is the cross not something that to the horror of others became scandalously visible precisely in its obscurity? Is it not visible enough that Christ is rejected and must suffer, that his life ends before the city gates on the hill of shame?[10] Is this invisibility?

It is in *this* light that the disciples' good works are to be seen. It is not you, but your good works that others should see, Jesus says. What are these good works that can be seen in this light? They can be no other than those Jesus himself created in them when he called them, when he made them into the light of the world beneath his cross: poverty, life as a stranger, gentleness, peaceableness, and finally also persecution and rejection, and in all this especially one thing, namely, to bear the cross of Jesus Christ. The cross is the peculiar light that shines and in which alone all these good works of the disciples can be seen. None of this says anything about God becoming visible. It is the "good works" that are meant to be seen, so that over them people give glory to God. The cross becomes visible, and the works of the cross become visible. The poverty and renunciation of the blessed become visible. In view of the cross and such a community of faith, however, it is no longer humankind that can be praised, but God alone. If these good works were actually human virtues, then glory would be given to the disciples themselves rather than to God. As it is, however, there is nothing to praise in the disciples who bear the cross, or in the community of faith whose light thus shines and that stands visibly on the hill—in view of their "good works" it is alone the Father in heaven who is praised. Thus do they *see* the cross and the congregation of the cross and believe God. That, indeed, is the light of the resurrection.

From: "The Sermon on the Mount. Matthew 5," in [The Cost of] *Discipleship*
Preliminary version: London 1934/1935
Final version: Finkenwalde 1936/1937

God in the
Midst of Life

Matthew 28:20: And remember, I am with you always, to the end of the age.

Fairy tales and legends from primeval times tell of the days when God walked among human beings. Those were splendid times, times when one encountered a stranger on the road seeking shelter; at home one recognized in this simple man the Lord God, and then was richly rewarded.[1] Splendid times, when God was so close to human beings that they could walk and speak with him. Indeed, times known only from fairy tales and legends, which speak of all the secret hopes slumbering in human beings as if all this were already reality. The beginning of our own Bible also tells us how the Lord God walked about in the evening in that garden in paradise and lived and spoke with human beings. Probably only very few peoples do not tell stories of such times. Blessed indeed were those permitted to experience such times when God and human beings were so close.

But how quickly things changed. Our Bible tells us the story of the Fall as the turning point in history.[2] Human beings were driven from the garden where they had lived with God, and now lived separated from God in guilt and unhappiness that increased with each succeeding generation. The fissure between God and human beings became ever greater; humanity submerged in the night. And as far as anyone can remember, human beings can speak only of this time of night, a time when God no longer goes about among human beings, and many a longing gaze turns back to the primeval age of fairy tales, to paradise, as if to a lost homeland one never really knew. Or men of mighty hope speak and spoke about coming days when God would once again dwell among human beings, when the Kingdom of God would be established on earth. God and human beings somehow belong together. God will return and once again be the guest of human beings.

There was one day in human history when this hope was radically thwarted, a day that forced us to become aware of the eternal distance between human beings and God—the day when humankind raised its hand against the God who wanted to dwell among them and nailed Jesus Christ to the cross: Good Friday. But there was also a day of divine response to human action, the day when God took up dwelling anew and for all eternity among human beings, the day when humankind's raised, unholy hand was filled with divine grace against all hope, the day when Jesus Christ was resurrected: Easter. Remember, I am with you always; that is the message of Easter. Not the distant God, but the God near to us; that is Easter.

Our own age is permeated by a searching, an anxious groping and asking for divine things. A great loneliness has descended upon our age, loneliness one finds only where one has been abandoned by God. The midst of our large cities, the scene of the most profuse, wild doings of the numberless human crowds. The great anguish of lonely isolation and homelessness has invaded. Yet the longing grows for a time when God will again linger among us, a time in which God can again be found. A thirst for contact with divine things has come upon human beings, a thirst burning hot and yearning to be quenched. And a great many remedies are being offered for sale today, promising radically to quench that thirst, drugs for which hundreds of thousands of greedy hands are reaching. And yet in the midst of all this wild commotion and quackery praising new remedies and treatments there stands the *one* word of Jesus Christ:

Remember, I am with you. . . . You do not need to search or to inquire or to carry on all sorts of hocus-pocus, for I *am* here. That is, Jesus does not say that he will someday come, nor is he prescribing ways one might get to him. Rather, he says quite simply: I am here. Whether we see him or not, feel him or not, want him or not makes no difference against the simple fact that Jesus is with us, that he is everywhere we ourselves are, and that we cannot contribute to that in the least. I am with you always. . . . And if this is indeed so, if Jesus really is with us, then God is with us. Wherever we ourselves might be, we are no longer abandoned, homeless, lonely. In that case—let us follow this to its conclusion—in that case, the time of legends has again become reality, and God is dwelling in our midst. Our only task is to keep our eyes open that we might recognize God—just as the people in the legend were supposed to recognize the Lord God in the sojourning stranger. God wants to be with us. Do we want to make a liar out of God by refusing to believe this? God is yet among human beings despite Good Friday. Remember, I am with you always. . . .

But before we break out in excessive rejoicing, let us reflect seriously for a moment. What does it really mean that Jesus or God is with us? That God is in the world? Where and how do we have some sense of this? God lives, lives for the world, the world becomes full of God, is transfigured, receives meaning *sub specie aeternitatis*[3]—this is the message of Easter. But now we ask further: Where in the world and in my own life do I sense something of the fullness of God? And we answer that today, too, God yet walks among us, and we are able to speak with him; we are together with him; indeed, we walk along with him in the street, meet him in the stranger while we travel, in the beggar before our door. The world is God's world. Wherever we go, we meet God. Jesus Christ, the Resurrected, is with us. Remember, I am with you. . . .

But is all this not just metaphorical language? What can we

possibly mean when we say that Jesus is with us? Is it not just a generalized, undefinable feeling?

No indeed; it is an utterly clear matter. Jesus is with us in his words, and that means quite clearly and unequivocally he is with us in that which he wants and what he thinks of us. He is with us with his will in his words, and only in our intercourse with Jesus' words do we sense his nearness. Words, in fact, are the clearest and most distinct means of expression through which spiritual beings can touch one another. If we have a person's word, we know that person's will and indeed the whole person. If we have Jesus' word, we know his will and his whole person. Jesus' word is always one and the same, and yet is always different. He tells us: You are standing under God's love, God is holy and you, too, are to be holy. God will give you the Holy Spirit that you, too, will be holy. And he says this to each person at each moment in a different way. God's word is one thing for a child and quite another for a man, and then something else for a young boy or a girl, and yet something else for a man or a woman. And yet there is no age, no moment in life when Jesus' word has nothing to say to us. Our whole life stands under his word, is sanctified by his word. From the cradle to the grave, the word of the church accompanies us and places us under the certainty of the statement: Remember, I am with you. As a symbol of this, the church has placed the different periods of human life under the proclamation of God's word. [. . .]

Remember, I am with you. . . . This is the case *whether we want it or not.* Are there any moments at all when we might not want this? In which God's presence is a burden? We all know that, indeed, there are such moments; and these are the moments of God's judgment upon us. God is with us—suddenly this statement becomes transparent in its entire scope. If God is with us, but we are not with God, what then? Let us once more follow this line of thinking with utter seriousness to its conclusion. It is not some respected prominent person, nor a prophet, nor some prince of the earth who comes to us and abides with us. It is the prince of life and of the whole world; he is with us with his judgment and his demands on us. Will we be able to do justice to this? And whether we try to rise up against him or to defend ourselves against him, he is there, always, to the end of the age. The blissful idea that God has again taken up dwelling among human beings, that he again wants to lend meaning to human life, that the world is again filled with God—this idea becomes threatening and frightening, for it involves responsibility. Our lives and actions are not to be meaningless, but what if we spend our time in dullness and thoughtlessness? Every age has its divine purpose. What if we fail to attend to this? Every moment of our lives is related to God. What if we want to sense nothing of this? So an enormous burden is placed upon us as soon as we take this statement seriously: Remember, I am with you. . . . But where the task is from God, there God also gives and forgives. Where God's judgment is, there also is God's mercy. Would God have come into the world and lived within it in order to bring it to ruin? No, God wants to impart to the world as much of God's life as is desired. He wants to draw unto himself the lonely and all those who desire his life, offering them the blessed twosomeness of God. "I am with you always. . . ." God lives, lives in the world, lives for the world, gives it meaning and life, makes it our home, relates our life to eternity and neighborhood—that is the grace we may receive from this saying of Jesus.

But one more thing. One profound feature of the fairy tale of which we spoke is that it understands God as walking about as a human being among human beings. This promise of the fairy tale, too, has become reality. Jesus Christ is with us not only in lonely hours, but may encounter us in every step we take, in every person we meet: Remember, I am with you. . . . Every person may be Jesus Christ, God himself, who is addressing us. The other person, this puzzling, impenetrable Thou, reminds us of God's addressing of and demand on us. It is the holy God himself who encounters us. The sojourner along the way, the beggar at the door, the sick person before the church door may represent God's demand on us, and no less so every person close to us, every person with whom we are together every day. Jesus says, "Just as you did it to one of the least of these, you did it to me."[4] I might represent for you and you might represent for me God's own demand on us, and with this realization our vision breaks through to the fullness of divine life in our world. Now life in the human community acquires its divine meaning. This community, this fellowship is itself a form of God's revelation. Whenever God is with us there is genuine community. This is the most profound meaning of our bonds to social life: That through it we are bound all the more firmly to God himself. Remember, I am with you always, to the *end of the age*. Again, the reference is to the ultimate things. "I am the first and the last," "Jesus Christ is the same yesterday and today and forever"—such are the words we hear.[5] Jesus is the Lord of the ages. He is with those who are his own always, even when things are hard. He will stay with human beings. That is our comfort. And should grief and anxiety come upon us, we may remember that Jesus is with us and will lead us over to God's eternal kingdom. Jesus Christ is the breadth of our life. Jesus Christ is the center of our community. Jesus Christ is with us to the end of the age, thanks to Easter.

Sermon
Barcelona, April 15, 1928 (First Sunday after Easter)

Notes

Back to the Cross

1. Cf. Ps. 121:1.
2. Cf. Ps. 104:2.
3. Luke 9:31.
4. Cf. v. 4 (Peter to Jesus); ". . . it is good . . . make dwellings" is an addendum at the bottom margin of the manuscript.

Discipleship and the Cross

1. Matt. 16:22f.
2. So for Paul, Rom. 6:6.
3. Instead of "If any . . . ," Luther follows a different reading in translating "Whoever . . ."
4. Matt. 26:74.
5. Cf. among the psalms of lament, e.g., Ps. 69:7f.: ". . . shame has covered my face. I have become a stranger to my kindred."
6. Heb. 13:12f.; cf. Lev. 16:10, 21f.
7. Luke 23:34, Jesus on the cross: "Father, forgive them . . ."
8. Matt. 10:24.
9. The *passiva* refers to the element of "must," that is, of having to suffer as opposed to choosing to suffer.
10. Martin Luther, *On Councils and Churches.*
11. 12th Schwabach Article (1529).
12. Cf. Matt. 27:46 (Jesus on the cross) with Ps. 22:1: "My God, my God, why have you forsaken me?"
13. Matt. 11:30.
14. Bonhoeffer cites according to K. Witte, *Luther-Andachten,* 243f.

(marked in Bonhoeffer's own copy), from Luther's second commentary to the seven penitential psalms.

Cain

1. Cf. John 4:14.
2. Bonhoeffer apparently cited from memory the final verse of the hymn "Praise God all Christians" by Nikolaus Herman (1500–1561), which actually reads "cherub" instead of "angel."

Judas

1. Cf. the announcements of suffering in Mark 8:31–33; 9:30–32; 10:32–34.
2. Cf. Matt. 26:20–25.
3. Matt. 26:40.
4. Matt. 26:56.
5. Cf. Luke 4:28–30; John 18:4–6.
6. Matt. 26:22.
7. Cf. John 6:70.
8. Cf. Matt. 10:1–8.
9. John 12:6.
10. Cf. John 13:26–30.
11. Matt. 26:24.
12. Cf. Rom. 11:1f., 11–16, 25–32.
13. Fifth strophe of the Passion hymn "O world, behold your life" (Paul Gerhardt, 1647).
14. Matt. 27:3–5.
15. The beginning of a strophe from medieval Passion and Easter plays, often used as a satirical song with which to poke fun at unpleasant foes. During the Reformation, Hermann Bonnus (1542) turned this satire into a penitential song ("O we poor sinners"). Cf. the *Handbuch zum Evangelischen Kirchengesangbuch* III/1, pp. 275–78.
16. Passion hymn (Michael Weisse, 1531).

Notes

Treasures of Suffering

1. See the date at the end of chapter.

Ecce Homo

1. Up to this point, the essay has sketched the basic outlines of the *"Führer*-democracy" of the Third Reich and of Hitler's perverted-plebiscitary rule. The text dates from 1940.
2. The expression "pariah," which has been taken over into English from Tamil, refers to groups who are repressed and scorned by the powerful.
3. In the hymn "Christ lay in the bonds of death," cf. the line ". . . swallowed death."
4. Cf. the Advent hymn "The night has advanced" by Jochen Klepper.
5. Cf. John 16:33.
6. Bonhoeffer wrote "scriptural references" in the margins here; for the published version, E. Bethge supplied the following passages: 2 Cor. 3:18; Phil. 3:10; Rom. 8:29, 12:2.
7. Cf. 1 Cor. 15:31.
8. From the hymn "Finally the hot crucible breaks" after K. F. Harttmann.
9. Phil. 1:21.

Resurrection

1. From the fourth verse of the hymn "Christ lay in the bonds of death."
2. Cf. Mark 15:34; Luke 23:46.
3. But cf. 1 Cor. 15:20–23.
4. Cf. Mark 16:5f. and parallels.
5. Cf. 1 Cor. 15:35ff.

Resurrection Instead of Immortality

1. Prometheus, the titan of Greek mythology, who represents human culture before Zeus, the highest God, and who must deceive God for the sake of that culture. With the onset of early dialectical

theology in the 1920s, Prometheus became the prototype of un-Christian cultural piety.

2. 1 Cor. 15:19. Actually: "If for this life only we have hoped in Christ, we are of all people most to be pitied."

Incarnation—Cross—Resurrection

1. 2 Cor. 5:17.
2. Rev. 21:5.

The Visible Community of Faith

1. Beginning in 1939, the evaluation of life as *"unworthy of life"* in the sense of the "Law for the Prevention of Descendants with Hereditary Diseases" (June 15, 1933) cloaked euthanasia activities in the Third Reich.
2. Cf. *Iliad* 9.214.
3. Matt. 15:24 and the commandment to evangelize in Matt. 28:18–20.
4. Martin Luther: "With the word *salt* he [Jesus] shows them what their [the addressees'] *office* is to be."
5. Cf. Martin Luther, Weekly Sermons on Matthew 5–7: There is no greater "ruin of Christendom than when the salt with which one must season and salt everything else itself loses its taste."
6. John 8:12.
7. "O Jerusalem, city built on high . . . ," a hymn modeled after Rev. 21:1–3 by Johann Matthaeus Meyfart (1590–1642).
8. English: "theology of the cross."
9. English: "civil justice."
10. Cf. Heb. 13:12f.

God in the Midst of Life

1. Allusion to the legend of Philemon and Baucis and similar stories.
2. Cf. Genesis 3.
3. English: "from the perspective of eternity."
4. Cf. Matt. 25:40.
5. Cf. Isa. 41:4; Rev. 1:11, 17; Heb. 13:8.